The Secrets of Advance Explosive speed kicking & Speed punching

By

Grand Master M. Jayanth Reddy

Winner of 29 Guinness World Records

PG PUBLICATION

Delhi - 110089, India

Edition : 2021

ISBN : 978-81-949743-3-8

The Secrets of Advance Explosive speed kicking
&
Speed punching

Cost : 1200/-

Published by
Prakhar Goonj Publication
H-3/2, Sector - 18,
Rohini, Delhi - 110089
Contact : 7982710571, 7838505899, 011-27851059
Email : prakhargoonj@gmail.com
sinha.neelu123@gmail.com

web : https://prakhargoonjpublicationofficialwebsite.com

The Secrets of Advance Explosive speed kicking
&
Speed punching

Dedication

This book is dedicated to my mother Late. Smt. M. Shivamma and my father Late Sri. M. Vithal Reddy

I thank my brothers, who inspired me to seek the wisdom of Martial Art Health, Wellness and longevity for the benefit of the whole world.

Finally I thank Mr. Anil vuchi who made this book page making and typed.

Phone: 0091-9391007598

Email: mjayanthreddy03@gmail.com

<u>**Table of Contents**</u>

Page No:

Saturday – 1st week

1. Tube kicking with single leg

Sunday – 1st week

1. Speed Under Water Kicks & Under Water Punche
2. Squats Kicks

2nd week schedule 68-105

Monday –2nd week

1. Ankle (Leg) Weights Kicks
2. Hand Weights

Tuesday – 2nd Week

1. speed peddle kicks(kicking on pad)

Wednesday-2nd week

1. speed nylon / tube kicking
2. speed kicking on pad with tieing tube
3. speed training of punches

Saturday – 2nd week

1. Tube kicking with single leg

Sunday – 2nd week

1. Speed Under Water Kicks & Under Water Punche
2. Squats Kicks

3rd week schedule 106-143

Monday –3rd week

1. Ankle (Leg) Weights Kicks
2. Hand Weights

Tuesday – 3rd Week

1. speed peddle kicks(kicking on pad)

Wednesday-3rd week

1. speed nylon / tube kicking
2. speed kicking on pad with tieing tube
3. speed training of punches

Saturday – 3rd week

1. Tube kicking with single leg

Sunday – 3rd week

1. Speed Under Water Kicks & Under Water Punche
2. Squats Kicks

6th week schedule 220 -257

Monday –6th week

1. Ankle (Leg) Weights Kicks
2. Hand Weights

Tuesday – 6th Week

2. speed peddle kicks(kicking on pad)

Wednesday-6th week

1. speed nylon / tube kicking
2. speed kicking on pad with tieing tube
3. speed training of punches

Saturday – 6th week

1. Tubc kicking with single leg

Sunday – 6th week

1. Speed Under Water Kicks & Under Water Punche
2. Squats Kicks

7th week schedule 258 -295

Monday –7th week

1. Ankle (Leg) Weights Kicks
2. Hand Weights

Tuesday – 7th Week

1. speed peddle kicks(kicking on pad)

Wednesday-7th week

1. speed nylon / tube kicking
2. speed kicking on pad with tieing tube
3. speed training of punches

Saturday – 7th week

1. Tube kicking with single leg

Sunday – 7th week

1. Speed Under Water Kicks & Under Water Punche
2. Squats Kicks

8th week schedule

296- 333

Monday –8th week

1. Ankle (Leg) Weights Kicks
2. Hand Weights

Tuesday – 8th Week

2. speed peddle kicks(kicking on pad)

Wednesday-8th week

1. speed nylon / tube kicking
2. speed kicking on pad with tieing tube
3. speed training of punches

Saturday – 8th week

1. Tube kicking with single leg

Sunday – 8th week

1. Speed Under Water Kicks & Under Water Punche
2. Squats Kicks

PREFACE

All the literature and scientific research information on the martial arts world, I have included very easy to understand from beginners to advanced level.
As you all understand the public has a growing interest in martial arts in every town to city or country.

Today, there are about 250 countries which are practicing martial arts worldwide, Chinese style, Japanese style, Korean style, Russian style, Philippines style, Thailand style, Indianstyle, European style are also growing worldwide. This book is helpful to all styles of martial arts worldwide to improve their kicking speed, power punch, stamina, endurance, skill, sparring techniques and various other standards of fitness and flexibility, agility and mind power to achieve world level competitions and Olympic events in martial arts.

Every technique is unique. Top coaches, fitness trainer, Physios, and psychologist and various styles of martial arts grandmasters have shared the winning secrets with me. Every chapterI technique I teaching method in this book is backed by the latest research, translated by me into plain English. Breakthrough methods developed from Elite training programs are made available to you through this book. Real and practical training for improving martial arts performance and avoiding injury, with clear illustrations, step by step workouts, exercise and advanced level of martial arts skills coupled with world champion techniques are incorporated in this book for you.

This is a rare book on the martial arts fitness. I intend to motivate and prepare you to practice the most advanced level of martial art techniques and exercises to improve whatever style you are in - get benefit out of most valuable information you have ever received earlier for this price.

No more time wasted on decades of practice strolling through unreliable information on the Internet, no more worry on different styles of martial arts emphasizing on traditional way of those forms, techniques which do not concentrate on inner body and Outer body which ultimately the performance is all about.

No more waste of time doing the wrong kind of training.

No more wastage of time hunting. You have seen enough. Many Grand Masters of various martial arts experts will convince you that you need S of training and spend untold legends of dollars I pounds I rupees to suck you into learning whatever style or system they are pushing. But, contrary to what they claim, you only need a handful of techniques combined with the right training and tactics to spar in any International competition or to protect yourself. You will have only 1I4 seconds to identify a threat and reactive or spar in competition in an offensive world. These are techniques that are simple and don't require a lot of time to master and make use of your core strength and power combined with the right tactics and training.

I wish you to be the most successful person on this planet.
This is the kind of high-level information that is kept to only a closed circle of top champions of martial arts, grandmasters, masters.
I hope to see you among the top professional coaches, master, champions and winners who use these techniques of this book and get very best results and helping you become the best you can be.

10 Commandments of real speed

by Grandmaster M Jayanth Reddy

1. Real speed is that you don't seek or get from others
2. Real speed is that you get when you practice
3. Real speed is that you are not afraid of others speed
4. Real speed is that your neuro's play Prime rule in speed training
5. Real speed is that you are very confident of participating in the championship
6. Real speed is that you know what you are and how you are
7. Real speed is that you don't compare with others
8. Real speed is that you know in how many seconds you knock out in the Championship
9. Real speed is that you don't bother about any techniques
10. Real speed is that you don't see what level of competition you are in

AUTHOR'S NOTE

With this Explosive training in speed kicking and speed punching, I have provided you with several exercises, schedule conditioning drills, and routines, I encourage you to review all of the exercises. Remember the famous words that variety is the spice of life. Do not perform the same exercises and routines each workout. Mix things up, be creative, dynamic schedule.

My experience and observations tell me that the majority of martial artist stick with the same routines. They are unwilling to expand their repertoire of exercise selection. You must realize that you are limiting your potential by neglecting exercise variety. Always keep your muscles guessing. Learn to shock your muscles in different ways.

You should make your quest for optimal fitness a lifelong mission. You must continually search for new ways to improve your condition, Experiment and use your brain. Too many martial artist today wish to be spoon-fed, rather than think for themselves. You must exercise your mind as well as your body if you truly wish to be successful (in competion and in speed kicking and speed punching).

As mentioned before, the schedules in this book are very strenuous. The conditioning drills are going to challenge you. There is no question about that. These schedules are designed to challenge you physically and mentally.

There will the mornings when you are sprinting the roads while the rest of the world sleeps. Your legs will fatigue as your wind runs short. It is at this point in time that you will determine how bad you wish to succeed. It is very easy to stop running, to turn around, and return home.

ANYONE can stop, only a select few will continue to work through the fatigue. Only a select few will ever become the "best" in speeding.

I do not wish to make these statements to discourage you or offend anyone. I am just stating the facts. I want you to read these words and ask yourself the question, "How bad do I want it?"

I cannot answer this question for you No one can but you. There will be days when you lack motivation, this is no reason to quit. We all go through ups and downs. Real champions persevere through hard times. Real champions never quit. Real champions overcome obstacles to become the best.

Whether you compete in an organized sport or not, you owe it to yourself to be the best that you can be. You can either view the glass as half empty of half full. You only have one chance to live your life. Live your life with energy. Live your life without regrets. If you have goals (and you should), go after them with relentless desire. Never "settle" for mediocrity.

Live your life by following the concept of CONTINUOUS IMPROVEMENT. Remember that the "best" is a moving target. Keep yourself heading in the right direction. Stay focused and go for the gusto!

I have witnessed countless martial artist that never lived up to their "potential" . These martial artist will one day contemplate what could have been or what should have been.

I wrote this book as a speedest man. My ultimate intent is to teach you to condition your body and mind in speed I have given you the tolls to improve your explosive and ability. Now I want you to take the ball and run with it. The fact that you purchased this Book tells me that me that you want to improve your performance. Remember that the journey is never ending. You can never settle because another hungry warrior is always eager to take your place at the top of the mountain.

Stay hungry, live life without regrets, and never look back.

In this book you can have the ultimate Workout program!

A program that gets you maximum results in minimum time. A program that builds incredible speed, definition, and power (any or all, it's up to you!). a program that doesn't injure your lower back, or destroy your knees, or overstress your other joints. A weekly program that will make you the best Explosive kicker you can be- or if you prefer, build you a phenomenal conditioning foundation for other martial arts including kickboxing, mauy thai ect.

This course weekly schedule unlocks the secrets of that ultimate program.

Secrets of Advance Explosive kick and punch: is the result of 20 years of research conducted by me experiencing my Guinness achievement to some of the best – known martial artist in the world. It synthesizes, into a coherent whole, information from many sources: interviews with successful master's and Grand masters studies performed on speed kick and speed punch and other players and the laws of kinesiology (the scientific study of the mechanics of human movement).

It works. Because it is specific. The research behind the program was aimed not only at determining which exercises are most effective, but more importantly, at discovering the optimum way to perform and combine them. This is **Synergism:** creating a whole greater than the sum of the parts. The individual exercises described become many times more effective when used exactly as indicated. **It is the details of performance, and the specific sequence schedule and timing that makes this program such a powerful conditioning tool.**

Secrets begin with an explanation of the biomechanical basis for the special techniques. First, it explores concepts behind optimum speed training. Then it moves on to concepts concerning speed training combination – how to structure your workout to maximize results (which kick or punch when, how many sets,repes,days ect. how to put togaether an intense, but short routine how to guarantee that each kick or punch your workout makes every other kick even more effective. This technical material is vital, because it give you the tools you need to understand, monitor, and update your program – to fine tune it to your personal needs and goals.

Next come illustrated descriptions of the speed training included in our routines. These also sever to illustrate the guidelines discussed in detailed. The descriptions are arranged by each and every kick and punch are discussed in prior ones). Secrets explores special training information related to each kick and punch and explains in detail how to optimize speed each of the weekly training schedules.

Following the exercises, we come to the routines.

Here, you will find 8 weeks complete program, each progressing from beginning to advanced. Although they have different goals, each in its own way is designed to get you maximum results in minimum time. Finally in "How Much, How Often, "this weekly course covers organizing your program in to a 7 days schedule (different method of speed training on different days), these Advance Explosive 8 weeks schedule as for all age groups are arranged training schedule according to the guidelines of many research and Experience of grand masters advice.

It can be altered only timings i.e the morning or evening according to each individual fit or adjustable but remember all 7 days a week scheduled cannot be altered, the speed training exercises. I hope with this secret training method will do justice for your training.

A NEW SCIENCE OF SPEED

* ***"This Book is dynamite"*:** It will blow and Blast through to Total Explosive Speed.

* **"This Book is a compass":** It will guide you into New worlds of speed kicking, speed punching.

* ***"This Book is a key"*:** It will open the door to all martial artist, masters and students dreams and develop the hidden potential.

* ***"This Book will work miracles"*:** It will open the eyes of all styles of martial artist, improve fighting, Dynamism a new courage of speediest fighter with speediest kicker and puncher.

Open your mind experience the Dynamic speed possiblities and you will never felt before and you can experience with your body response with this new science of speed. Remember. Don't listen to all of the stylish martial arts and infomercials ect. That claim that their stylish martial arts are the best in the world, there is no single best method I have mentioned lots of re-researched information for fit into individual of male and female and children accordingly scheduled for best in the world.

You know I am 50 year old can achieved speediest kicker and speediest puncher in the world Honoured by Guinness world Records. This science on speed kicking and speed punching helped me why not everyone you may not be a follower of science but must not ignore the facts when I train my self or anyone I take care of training with hard core, no nonsense approach. If you want to be the world's best kicker or puncher, you are going to have to bust your ass no magic pill or power will get you to the world top speedest kicker or puncher if you are not willing to work hard.

To be the best you will need to train hard and overcome all fatigue, strain during the Journey of the goal.

While I am busting my ass training, scientist sit in their laboratories trying to make sense of the most complex system in the world of research, the human body. The human body is an amazing creation. There are no limitations on our ability. The ultimately the key to success is a combination of hard work and intelligent training.

Forget about what someone did or supposedly did 100 or 200 years ago. The fact remains that today's martial artist is bigger, stronger and faster than ever before. Advancements have been made that must not be ignored.

The point that speed training I wish to convey is that you need to bust your ass and expand your full energy in the most productive manner possible. A warrior within yourself must train hard and come out as intelligent as possible.

These secret speeds training with its proven physiological and psychological technology will motivate, guide and inspire you to reach your full potential in your martial arts world.

This secret of underground Guide to speed kicking and speed punching informative training program together to help every individual martial artist to become a warrior speed.

The Book will teach you to be resourceful and creative in your quest for physical and mental speed in martial arts whether you are competitive martial artist or just for a self defence or fitness learner you will learn how to revolutionize your martial art workout conveniently with easy schedules.

If you purchased this book expecting an effort less workout, I suggest that you read no further and submit a refund request from Author.

SECRET OF SPEED TRAINING SCHEDULE

At this point, I have provided you with several exercises methods and speed conditioning drills. If you combine these exercises with a weekly plan, you are on the road to explosive speed.

Notice that i use the words "if you" follow these routines... Anyone can purchase this book and memorize the exercises and weekly advice. Simply reading through the book will not make you a explosive speed If you truly want to be the best, you must prepare yourself for a long journey of hard work and dedication.

Forget about whether or not you participate in any formal, martial art competitions. We are all competitors. You should compete with yourself each and every day. You should approach each day as an opportunity to improve yourself. You can improve strength, speed, power, intelligence, morality, or any other characteristic of your life.

Too many people piss away their lives. The elderly often look back on their life with regrets. Do not let this happen to you. There is no excuse to live with regrets. If you have goals (which you should), no one can stop you on your journey except yourself. If you want to be the best, make the decision today to dedicate yourself to hard work and perseverance. The routines in this book are difficult. They will challenge you physically and mentally. Accept and overcome the challenge. Wake up each day knowing that you are a road on warrior speed.

These routines will give you a whole new level of "power" in life. We all know the old mantra, "mind over matter"... These routines will bring these words into your life. Anyone who can do 1000 consecutive Ankle weight kicks possesses far more than physical power. The warrior who achieves these physical feats does so by drawing energy from a powerful mind. We have all been told, "you can do anything that you put your mind to... Why do so few people actually live up to these words?

The answer is simple. It takes hard work and discipline to fulfil your potential.

We all have the opportunity to be the best, yet very few of us make the sacrifice to go for it. When I say, "be the best", I am referring to your best. Be the best that you can be in competition, at work, at home, or wherever and whatever you pursue. Second place sucks. Do not "settle" for anything. Make the decision that you will emerge as a top

Why do you think there are so many martial art styles equipments gadgets and magic pills? The organizations that market these items understand the population. They know how to target the masses. The masses are weak. The masses search for the easy way out. The masses are not truly successful. The heck with the masses and mediocrity. You have the opportunity to differentiate yourself from the rest of the crowd. Take advantage of this opportunity.

MOTIVATION

One of the most common question I am asked is, “How do you stay motivated?”
I usually respond to this question with my own question. How the heck do you allow yourself to lose motivation? How do you live with yourself knowing that you only gave a half ass effort? There is no secret to motivation, whether towards training or life in general. You need to be motivated to live. You need to view life as an opportunity. I cannot stand those people who waste their days feeling bad for themselves. Life is a big opportunity. Get off your ass and go for it.

We have all heard stories about a man (or woman) who came to this country with nothing but the shirt on their back. Ten years later this person is one of the most successful businessmen in the world. There is no magic involved with these stories, just hard work, perseverance, and sacrifice. There are no magic equations to success. Once you make the decision, there is nothing that can stand in your way.

In terms of the explosive, training program, I can only show you how to perform the exercises. I can proved you with the workouts and routines but I am NOT at your side to ensure that you work your hardest. No one can make that decision for you.

DO NOT SKIP WORKOUTS

Let’s face it, as human beings we are going to have good days and bad days. No matter your motivation towards life, there are days when you will be challenged. You may be tired or sore and do not want to train. Maybe you stayed out late one night and do not want to run the next morning. Your mind will start talking shit to you, encouraging you to go back to sleep.
When you miss one workout, it becomes much easier to skip another. Before you know it, you convince yourself to start over next Monday. Do not get into this habit for some reason everyone wants to start on Monday. The heck with Monday! Start your training program today! You must make the decision for yourself as to how successful you want to be. I cannot make that decision for you.

FEELING SORE?

The routines in this training scheduled will leave you sore. This is a fact which we must come to terms with. I still get sore to this day I have been following many of these routines for several years. Soreness should give you a reason to skip your workout, right? WRONG. Not every workout will be most intense day of training. If your legs are extremely sore from yesterday's workout, lighten the load and focus more on your upper body or midsection, when one muscle group is sore, you can always work another part of your body. Low intensity work may actually help to alleviate the soreness by clearing up the lactic acid that has built up in your muscles.

BE INTELLIGENT

I have provided you with several exercises methods of speed kicking and speed punching and conditioning drills, and routines. These routines will give you a good start on your journey to the land of explosive speed with this said, there is nothing stopping your from "thinking outside the box". Do not be a "yes man", meaning someone who simply does as he is told without thinking for himself. I encourage you to develop your own routines. Keep things interesting by incorporating variety into your training regimen. Make it your mission to devise new exercises and routines that will help you achieve your goals.

Another important piece of advice is to plan your workouts ahead of time. Do not approach your workout with no idea what you will do. Plan ahead of times so you can move quickly from one exercise to the next.

KEEP A WORKOUT LOG

Keep track of your progress. Monitor your results with a workout log that lists your personal bests. If you can do 500 speed kicks a day, write it down. In a few weeks you can look back at the log and realize the improvements that you have made. By doing so, you will not just "think" that you have improved, you will have proof on paper. After a few months, you will be surprised at the improvements that you have made. I GUARANTEE it! My Experience says.

MORINING OR NIGHT?

Do not worry about what time of the day you train. A could ramble on about what time of the day your body produces optimum ratios of anabolic and catabolic hormones but it does not matter. Forget about morning, noon, afternoon, or evening. Just be sure that you find time, whatever time that may be. You can even break your workout into different times morning and evening.

HOW MANY DAYS PER WEEK?

My Elite schedules have to train 7 days per week, 365 days per year. You can exercise every day as long as you do so intelligently. You must balance your moderate intensity days with maximum intensity sessions. Warriors speed training must train hard but also train smart. Over – training will lead to excessive muscular burnout and breakdown. It is a good idea to use one day per week for rest. I typically "rest" on Sunday. My "rest" day usually consists of some walking, stretching, and light shadow sparring there is no reason to sit around all day a couch potato. Most importantly, listen to your body. No one knows your body better than YOU. If you are completely beat down, there is no shame in taking some time to rest and recuperate.

LET'S GET STARTED

No it is time to look at some specific training routines. Once again, these routines are not etched in stone. You can make adjustments where necessary. There is no shame if you cannot complete the number of prescribed repetitions / scheduled take it one day at a time. Patience is a virtue. You body cannot be built over night. Productive change takes time.

Once you have read through this chapter you will have all the tools necessary to become a warrior speed you must take the initiative to use these tools. I have done my part, now the rest is up to you. Take the ball and run with it.

You can do ANYTHING that you put your mind to. Ask yourself what you wish to accomplish, why did you buy this Book? Once you have determined your answers, you must develop a course of action that will lead you to your goals. The warrior's speed training routine will show you the path. It's up to you to follow the schedule.

THE TRAINING ROUTINES

In the Routines section, we explored the guidelines for optimizing speed training exercise one effective way to use this course is to modify the exercises in your own routine based on those guidelines. That alone should lead to a substantial increase in the effectiveness of your training in the weekly program.

Of course, there's no reason to stop at optimum speed training performance. Proper exercise sequence takes you even further along the path toward the perfect program.

In this Routine section we combine the exercise from the first section into a series of routines of 8 weeks ranging from simple to complex – designed to give you maximum results in minimum time. The routines are also intended to illustrate the concepts of optimizing speed training exercises sequence, and can be used as templates, or patterns, from which to design more individualized routines. By following the instructions in this schedule, you should be able to construct the ultimate program for you, tailored to your own needs, goals, and body structure.

I am going to present 3 different approaches to applying the exercises sequence guidelines for above 15 years, 13 years to 15 years and below 13 years schedules routine.

This individual routines for each kick and punch are optimized according to the sequence guidelines and then the speed training workout is ordered according to the Interdependency principle. This is an advanced, powerful explosive program that will generate incredible gains. Choose an approach according to your need if possible or if you wish.

WARM UP

1).Warm up first: Regardless of whether you are going to lift weight or throw two hundred punches or kicks you have to make the transition between inactivity and exercise gradually.

A warm –up consists of three parts: limbering up, cardio-vascular warm – up, and specific muscular warm – up

Limbering up is not the same as stretching to increase flexibility. It involves going through a short series of stretching exercises without pushing yourself. Limbering up is the first step in the transition between inactivity and exercise.

For the cardiovascular warm-up, you can use anything that gets your blood pumping running, riding a stationary (or non- stationary) bike, jumping jack, running in place, etc. This is stage two.

Finally, you need to prepare your muscles and joints for the specific activity in which you are about to engage. If you are going to punch the heavy bag, throw some easy punches in the air same as kicks if you are going to do ankle weights, kicks pick up a pair of very light Air kicks and run through the exercises from your routine.

2.)Do exercises that involve the different muscle on the same days. For example if you're going to do ankle weight kicks and punches in the evening. As –a result, your legs and hands get to rest and recover accordingly.

I have combining different workouts in different days thoroughly warm up the lower body, decreasing your risk of injury, it also pre-exhausts the legs, allowing you to get maximum growth using less weight. (Remember it's not the amount of weight you put on ankle or hands that counts, it's the Fatigue/Tension level developed in the muscle.)
Here are some other combinations of exercises that use the same basic muscle, and should be performed on the same day.

- Martial arts kicking/lower body work
- Martial arts punching /upper body work

3). **Finally: stretch as late in your routine as possible.** Stretching is not a warm – up exercise! Pushing to increase your flexibility when you are cold is like flattening out a rusty hinge with a hammer. It creaks and groans, and won't open very far anyway.

The best time to stretch is after you finish day schedule. All that pumping is like putting oil on the hinge. In fact, if you stretch after day schedule, you will develop more flexibility more quickly, experience much less of the pain usually associated with stretching, and suffer less soreness from your ankle and hand and tube workout!

We strongly recommend you include upper and lower body stretch routines at the end and beginning of your schedule.

- Warm up before engaging in any physical activity.
- Do different kinds of exercises that involve the different muscles on the same days, preceded by specific warm - ups.

CAUTION

SPEED TRAINING FOR WHITE BELT OR BEGINNER

If you are a beginner, you must know the kicks and punches perfect by further you focus every muscle flexibility strength to bear loads on ligaments, instead of focusing on isolation exercise intend to get you in touch right away with how it show feel to work each muscle group in speed training in speed kicking and speed punching and also the numbers of reps, schedules on this level are higher other optimum for promoting speed this limits the amount of ankle weight and hand weight you can use, giving your body a chance to adapt to the rigours of speed training. The idea is to take it slow and build a solid foundation for fort future development as you are beginner you first start out, perform only flexibility, strength in hands and legs and basic kick perfection then you can start with a minimum repetition as I mention the schedule according to age.

IMPORTANCE OF BODY COOL DOWN EXERCISE

In this speed Book there are several Exercise and methods mentioned are cautioned to beware of the straining and tearing that can result without proper limbering and stretching exercise in executing many these kicks methods mentioned even an otherwise relatively accomplished martial artists can expect difficulty and frustration unless he takes time to warm up. The main purpose of the warm-up is to increase blood circulation to raise general body and deep muscle temperatures. In doing so, you warm up your muscles, ligaments and tendons in preparation for more vigorous activity. A proper warm-up will reduce your chance of injury, improve performance, and increase your range of motion and elasticity. In addition, the warm-up increases muscular or efficiency, improves reaction time and improves the speed of kicks and movements of muscles and ligaments.

Warm-up and warm down (cool down) is as important as warm –up unfortunately many martial artits fail to properly cool down following a practice session. Cool down muscles will do wonders to reduce fatigue and soreness in various parts of the body.

I always see people realize that after they feel exhausted after an intense martial Arts practice session their exhaustion often results in their minds telling that to forget about the cool down (warm down). As a warrior you need to suck it up and finish your cool down period. The few minutes that are required will save your many hours of soreness and fatigue.

HYPNOSIS IN MARTIAL ARTS

Developing martial arts through hypnosis: First you must learn the basics of martial arts. The correct methods to block, kick, punch and correct strategies and tactics and then only mind will accept. Otherwise, it won't improve.

Sit comfortably and firmly in a relaxed position, with both your feet flat on the floor and your arms on the arms of the chair. Close your eyes, take a deep breath in and out then start count from 100 to 1 after count of one you are totally relaxed into subconscious mind. This is the first method and second method is self talk and third is progressive relaxation.

Self-Talk to yourself in Positive:

Self-talk means talk is not just verbal; it is feeling that self of positive or negative. We have to be certain that positive thinking bring everyone that they desire. Obviously many hear negative on their performance in martial arts and get disturbed and grow and be reinforced by that negative internal talk (feelings). Unless we make an effort to stop the negative process at the outset as soon as a negative thought arises that changes your behaviour or physioclogically.

Unless we empower with the positive attitude like - 'I am strongest man on this earth and feel with confident'. This affirmation will always put you in dominating negative.

Fee that if you lose this competition, how you will be criticized or degraded. Think your rigorous practice that you have, bloodshed practice of years will be waste.

Furthermore we will not be using the phrases - I am weak or fearful of any competition; instead we should use the words or feelings that - I am, I am powerful.

Progressive Relaxation:

This is general relaxation method. Have the person to be hypnotized adjust himself comfortably hypnotized either sitting or lying down. Then proceed as follows:

Record it Audio tape or do it remembering every part of body. "Close your eyes and let yourself become as relaxed as possible. Just let yourself go. Let all the tension drain out of your body. Listen to my voice and pay no attention to anything else. Relax and listen to my

Voice. And as you do so, you will become even more and more relaxed that you will go into a hypnotic trance, a peaceful, deep, relaxing sleep

"Now focus your attention on you head. Let muscles of your head become completely relaxed. Let all the tension flow out of- your head. And your head becomes loose and relaxed.

And the wonderful relaxation flows down over your forehead and face, loosening and relaying the muscles of your forehead of your face. And the relaxation flows down the back of your neck, loosening up the muscles of your neck. And all the muscles of your neck are loose relaxed. Your jaw is loose and relaxed. "

"Now the wonderful relaxation spreads all over your body. The muscles of your shoulders become relaxed more and more relaxed. You feel the muscles of your back loosen up and become relaxed. You are becoming more and more relaxed. Your chest muscles are becoming loose and relaxed, allowing you to breathe more easily and more deeply. All the tension is draining out of your body".

Continue this pattern down the body, mentioning the muscles of arm, left biceps is loose and relax. Feel your biceps' is loose and relaxing. Go to the right bicep and left bicep is loose and relaxed. Your triceps is loose and relaxed. Elbows are loose and relaxed. Feel your elbow is loose and relaxed. Hands and fingers are loose and relaxed. Then feel that your hands and fingers are loose and relaxed. Feel this left and right sides. Abdomen is loose and relaxed. Then feel your abdomen is loose and relaxed. Your left leg is loose and relaxed. Feel your left leg is loose and relaxed. Same with the right leg. Your calf is loose and relaxed. Feel your left calf is loose and relaxed. Same with the right calf. Your left leg shin is loose and relaxed. Feel your left leg shin is loose and relaxed. Same with the right leg shin. Your left ankle is loose and relaxed. Feel your left ankle is loose and relaxed. Same with the right ankle. Your left foot is loose and relaxed. Feel your left foot is loose and relaxed. Same with the right foot. Repeat after 3 times of each and every part of muscle, loose and relax.

Use your own dialogue speaking in soothing gentle, rhythm. The technique can be as brief as you like, or as detailed as you feel necessary, according to how well the person responds. Finish the sequence of progressive relaxation with something like:

All tension is gone from your body. Your entire body is completely relaxed. More relaxed than it has ever been in a long, long' time. You no longer have any cares or worries for the moment. Continue to listen to my voice and enjoy the deep, wonderful relaxation.

Suggestion:

1. Enter into subconscious and then start giving the suggestions

I am increasing speed and power in my technique, feel, believe, believe and see actually that you are doing it

2. My reflexes and co-ordination becoming faster and better as my techniques become more automatic.

3. My ability of sparring is getting better and better every day. Repeat each about suggestion

for 5 to 10 times in subconscious.

Do it every day twice in the morning and twice in the evening; thrice would be even better.

After suggestions tell yourself that I will count from 1 to 5 at the count of 5 my eyes will open and be fully alert, and refreshed.

One: I am relaxed and calm.

Two: I am going to awake and feel alert. Three: I

am fully alert and feeling relaxed. Four: I am

relaxed and calm and alert.

Five: I am wide awake and feeling relaxed and refreshed.

The above method is very simple and can easily be learnt. Don't learn many things and mess it. Don't confuse the mind.

The about suggestions are designed for Martial artist who has had at least perfect basic movements of training experience. The suggestions can, and will enhance your overall development and performance, regardless of you were present ability level.

Remember that the change in your martial arts ability no not take place overnight but, there will be definite and noticeable change in two weeks' time. At first, you may not notice the change but others will. Your instructor workout partner and opponent will probably become aware of the change before you do.

Rest assured that if you follow the directions as given above progress will surely come. Do not modify or change the directions or suggestions. Do not forget, neglect, or skip twice a day everyday practice.

A great deal of thought has gone into making them as scientific and they will work for you - just like the martial arts themselves.

Rules of Giving Effective Suggestions:

1. Always use simple clear stated words and phrased to assure yourself and persons whom you understands the suggestions.

2. Always use positive wording never use negative, for ex: say I will or you will feel self- confident, but do not say t' you will no longer lack self Confidence.

3. Convey mental images as clearly as you can such as, you can see yourself talking confidently.

4. The sub-conscious should not be burdened with too many suggestions at one time or at the most two. The effect becomes diffused otherwise work with repetition of one or two suggestions for two or three reasons. If other ends are sought, use suggestions on another one or two for a few times, then go back and repeat the first ones.

5. Repeat mentally 5 to 8 times in sub-conscious with feel, believe, and see

Preparation Exercises for Hypnotism:

Take a sheet of white paper draw a circle with radius of 2 or 2½ "with dot in the center, and draw line of vertical and horizontal, Tie small object (an ear ring or any circular thing) on the end of- a length of thread. Have the person sit at table and hold this pendulum with thumb and index finger and bent wrist, over the dot on the paper. The person should be resting his elbow on the table and, the pendulum about half an inch above the dot. And concentrate on first horizontal line and it will move fast. Don't make it intentionally and then concentrate on vertical line and then circular each 1 minute you practice every day Morning and Evening. After week two you start with doing eyes also close your eyes, visualize the pendulum

Moving side to side. See it moving in your mind's eye. Visualize it just as realistically as you can (just the way to did in an early opening eyes). Then visualize up and down and then circular, open your eye see after side to side and the up and down. Circular you will know whether is moving or not: and also once you can obtain these 3 motions without help from your conscious mind. You improve lot of concentration and you can purify your subconscious mind.

The serious student of self-hypnosis can reshape his life, become more self-confident and motivated, remove fears and undesirable habits, and remake himself into the person he would truly like to be.

Where to Practice Self-Hypnosis:

You should practice where it's quiet and free of distractions, and comfortable.

Typically the most ideal place is the bedroom where one can lie down relax completely. Lighting and temperature should be comfortable so that no notice is given to these things. Sometimes slight noises are unavoidable and yet is distracting. To cover such noise soft music from FM radio can help make smoothing background that actually helps you to relax and promote self-hypnosis.

Before you settle down to routine training for self-hypnosis consider all possible sources of distractions and do what you can to eliminate them.

Attitude in Self Hypnosis:

Self-hypnosis is a scientific fact. Famous Fakirs and Yogis use it to meditate. Slow the heart rate. They know that self-hypnosis works. It will work for you too, when you have trained yourself sufficiently.

Accordingly you must adopt a positive attitude in your (mind that self-hypnosis will work for you...that is does work for you. This attitude is a psychological mental set ..a mental pattern of acceptance that is vital to enable you to learn hypnosis in the first place. This is. Perhaps the most basic subtle and important secret for successfully learning and applying self-hypnosis.

Training Time:

On the average, the most efficient training is two sessions per day lasting about fifteen minutes each session, practicing 7days each week. Under this training schedule the average student gets good, results within three or four weeks. Some learn quicker, and some need more time.

First Basic Technique: The first and quickest way to learn self-hypnosis is to have a professional hypnotist train you. The hypnotist will put you into a state of hypnosis as deep as possible and give you special post hypnotic suggestion to help you duplicate this mental state at your own will, whenever you desire.

A typical post hypnotic suggestion for this is:

Each time you wish to hypnotize yourself, you will be successful in reaching the desired state of hypnosis by yourself. And the suggestions that you desire to give yourself will be accepted by your unconscious mind and take the fullest effect.

Second Basic Technique: This technique has several variations. You record on a tape a complete hypnotic session, with all the hypnotic and post-hypnotic suggestions you desire. In this way your own voice becomes the hypnotist. You are hypnotized by yourself, by tape. You alter ego is hypnotizing you giving commands. Programming your inner mind the way you want. You are hypnotizing yourself by remote control by this method yet 'you' have complete control.

Third Basic Technique: This technique depends entirely upon your own skills ability to channel your thoughts into the proper sequence patter. It is a little hard way to learn self- hypnosis and thus requires more patience and persistence

SPEED TRAINING SCHEDULE V/S COOKING

Consider that world renowned chefs who have become famous for their tasty entrees and desserts. Each ingredient is selected with a specific purpose. The chef is careful to select the best ingredients. Each ingredient is precisely measured. Too much of one ingredient can ruin the recipe. Each meal is cooked for pre-determined time period. If the chef over cooks the meal. It will be ruined. Let's now relate these cooking term to our speed training program. Our ingredients are the speed training exercises that we include in our workout.

The quantity of each ingredient relates to the number of sets and repetitions that we perform for each speed training. Suppose a recipe calls for 1 cup of sugar, but the chef instead uses 1 teaspoon. Obviously he has not used enough sugar to generate a taste. The same logic applies to speed training. If our ingredient consists of kicks, but we only do 10 kicks, we have not used enough of this ingredient to generate a response. The ingredient is useless unless we use the correct quantity of 100 kicks of each kick is right number.

What about cooking time? If a meal is over cooked, if will be ruined. This concept also applies to speed training. If you "over cook" the muscles your recipe will be ruined. You must work the muscles without over training. If you "under cook" the muscles you have not trained hard enough. Hence will not generate a noticeable response.

Three important principles of speed training:

1. Select the kick of punch do with Ankle weight or drum bell in hand of 1 kg or 2kgs more or nylon tube.
2. Perform the minimum of 100 kicks or punch in each set.
3. Avoid over training (and under training)

WORD OF CAUTION TO STUDENTS AND MASTERS DURING ANKLE WEIGHT, KIT/ BAG OR SQUAT KICK PRACTICING OR NYLON TUBE KICKS

a. During kit bag workout never lock your knee during your Kick to kit bag. during any kick the knee should be bent during the hits

b. Never lock the knee when you are practicing ankle weight. It will damage the knee. Never practice kicks slow; the ankle weights kick is very speed.

c. Air kick should be pulled very fast. never use whole body to kick; speed kick as if you kick a paper are having a x-ray film

d. Squat kicking should not be pretty slow you should do it fast - getting up and kick. if you are exhausted after 10 or 20 repetitions take rest and do again

e. Ankle weights / kit bag workout should also be practiced without locking the knee. The hit must be observed by kit before locking

f. never lock elbow while punching on the kit bag while practicing punch with weight on a kit bag

g. while performing cycle tube kicking, for the kick to be powerful and devastating, - pulling obviously happens but you should continue to focus on kicks on the kicking pad

h. Never practice ankle weights kick and weight punch daily; you should allow the leg and hand to relax. Do it twice or thrice a week

i. 13 Years above can do tube kicking for boys or girls - maximum 500 kicks

j. 14 Years and above can do Ankle weight kicks – maximum 1000 kicks by boy and girls

k. 14 Years and 15 Years of boys and girls can do punches according to the above tube and weights rules

1st Week

Speed Training schedule for 15 Years and above

Speed Training schedule for 13 – 15 Years

Speed Training schedule for below 13 years

"The greatest asset of my physical ability and mental ability is my speed"

\- Grand Master M. Jayanth Reddy

SPEED TRAINING OF KICKS- 15 YEARS AND ABOVE

Monday –I 1st week schedule

½ kg ANKLE (LEG) WEIGHTS KICKS(Alternative Legs)

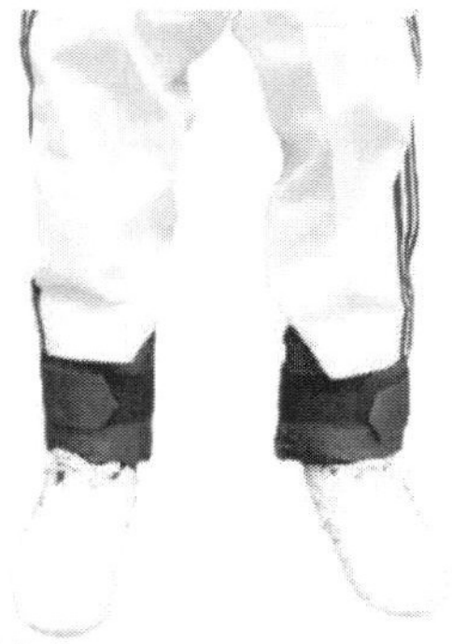

Wear a Ankle weight to your leg ½ kg each leg and start kicking all the kicks as shown in the pictures below. Each kick you need to do a minimum of 5 kicks each leg Rest for 30 seconds. Do all 1 to 10 kicks.

1. DOWN HEEL KICK, ALTERNATIVE LEGS

2. SIDE KICK, ALTERNATIVE LEGS

3. SPINNING CART WHEEL KICK, ALTERNATIVE LEGS

4. HOOK KICK, ALTERNATIVE LEGS

5. TRUST KICK ALTENATIVE LEG

6. INNER EDGE KICKS ALTERNATIVE LEGS 7. FRONT SIDE KICKS ALTERNATIVE LEGS

8. ROUND HOUSE KICK ALTERNATIVE LEGS

9. OUTER EDGE KICK ALTERNATIVE LEGS

10. BACK KICK AND DO ALTERNATIVE LEG

II. ½ kg of Ankle Weight kick Controlling:

Do only 4 Kicks i.e., (1) Thrust Kick (2) Side Kick (3) Round House Kick (4) Back Kick Control Each Leg at hips minimum do control for 5 to 8 seconds without any support. See Picture A,B,C and D. Do 2 sets each.

Pic-A
Thrust Kick, Alternative Legs

Pic-B

Side Kick, Alternative Legs

Pic-C

Round House Kick Alternative Legs

Pic-D

Back Kick do with Alternative Leg

III. Sitting kicks with ½ kg Ankle Weight :

Do only 4 kicks (1) snap kicks (2) Side kick (3) Round house kick (4) Hook kick.
Do each kick 25 times alternative legs Lie down on back and wear ½ kg Ankle weight and kick continuously snap kicks for 15 to 20 kicks see pic-P1 ,pic- P2 and p3.

Pic-P1

Pic-P2

Pic-P3

Kneel led down and sit and hands support on the ground and raise your Right leg Right side and kick side kick continuously 15 to 20 kicks with wearing ½ kg Ankle weights and change the leg and do with other leg same. See pic-P4 and pic-P5.

pic-P4

pic-P5

Kneel led down and sit and hands support on the ground and kick round house kick sideways 15 to 20 times each leg with wearing ½ kg Ankle weight. See pic-P6 and pic-P7

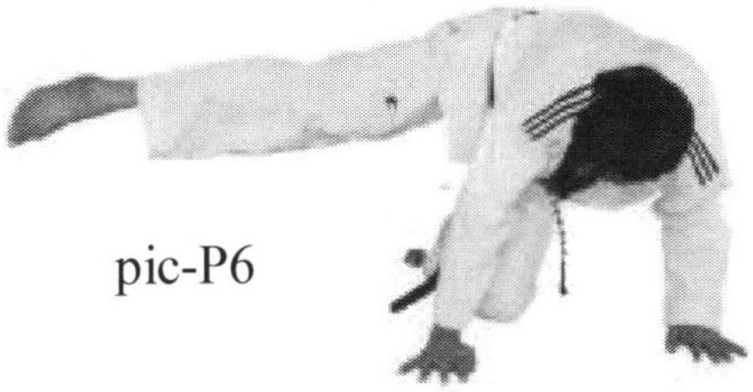

pic-P6

pic-P7

Kneel led down and sit and hands support on the ground and kick Hook kick sideways 15 to 20 times each leg wearing ½ kg Ankle weight. See pic-P8 and pic-P9.

pic-P8

pic-P9

SPEED TRAINING OF PUNCHES - 15 YEARS AND ABOVE

Monday –I 1st week schedule

½ kg HAND WEIGHTS (Alternative Hands)

(a) Horse stand Horse stand and hold ½ kg hand weight and Do 25 punches with alternative hands with ½ kg hand weight. See picture 1 and 2

Pic -1

Pic -2

(b) Stand in front forward stance and punch with single Right hand over the left open hand (Bend at elbow in the front) 25 punches with Single hand with ½ kg hand weight.
And change the hand i.e. change to left hand And punch with the same as Right hand punch.
See picture 3,4,5 and 6

Pic -3

Pic -4

Pic -5

Pic -6

(C) Speed sitting hand weights punches Sit on chair or stool and punch at least 25 times with alternative hand (with left hand and right hand)
Variation: your can do this sitting punches by blind folded i.e. with closing eyes, by imagining You are smashing with punch. See picture 7 and 8

Pic -7

Pic -8

Forearm Strengthening Exercises 1

Holding 12" to 15" long rod 3 pounds (approximately) tightly on the right side and twist 180degrees for 5 times and change the hand and continue. See pictures A, B, C
Variations: You can hold 2 rods either side of each hand and twist them.

Pic - A

Pic - B

Pic - C

Forearm Strengthening 2

Hold 12" to 14" rod 3 pounds (approximately) in front of you and twist left and right 180 degrees angle with left hand 5 times repetitions and change to right hand and do the same repetitions. See pictures A, B, C, D, E and F.

Pic - A Pic – B Pic – C Pic- D Pic – E Pic - F

Triceps Strengthening Exercise 3

Keep index and thumb of each hand join together and go for pushups with leg stretch out without bending knees. Do this exercise for 5 times daily. See pictures A and B.

Pic A

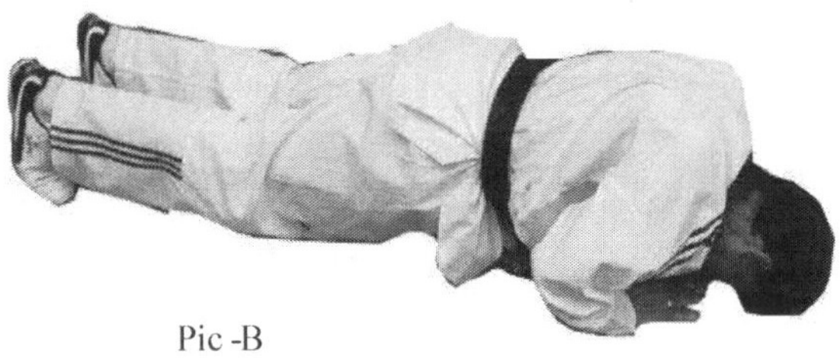

Pic -B

Friday: Same as on Monday Schedule

SPEED PEDDLE KICKS(kicking on pad)

Tuesday 1st week schedule

I. PAD KICKING EACH LEG 10 KICKS 1 TO 15 KICKS

(1) Push kick
(2) Front thrust kick
(3) Side kick
(4) Round house kick
(5) Back kick
(6) Outer edge kick
(7) Inner edge kick
(8) Down heel kick
(9) Hook kick
(10) Jumping side kick
(11) Jumping Round house kick
(12) Jumping Back kick
(13) Spin kick
(14) Jumping spin kick
(15) Scissor kick

Jumping thrust kick

Push Kick on Pad -1

Front thrust kick on pad -2

Side kick on pad -3

Round house on pad-4

Back kick on pad – 5

Outer edge kick on pad – 6

Inner edge kick on pad -7

Down heel kick on pad -8

Hook kick on pad – 9

Jumping side kick on pad – 10

Jumping Round house kick on pad - 11

Jumping Back kick on pad – 12

Jumping spin kick on pad - 13

Front Side kick -14

Scissor kick-15

II. PAD KICKING LEFT LEG 10 KICKS IN SINGLE LEG

III. PAD KICKING RIGHT LEG 10 KICKS IN SINGLE LEG

Note: I,II and III Rest for 1 minutes of each kick, Do all kicks accordingly

Thursday: Same as on Tuesday Schedule

SPEED NYLON / TUBE KICKING

Wednesday 1st week schedule

Speed Kicking With Tube

Tie bicycle tube or nylon thread and tie to your ankle and kick all kicks 10 times in 20 seconds alternative leg. Rest for 30 seconds with each kick.
Do all kicks below mentioned stationary kicks 10 kicks in 20 seconds and 5 jumping kicks in 15 seconds.

Speed Kicking With Tube

Tie bicycle tube or nylon thread and tie to your ankle and kick all kicks 10 times with each leg.
This improves kicking speed. Once in a week you can do single leg kick and alternative leg kicks.

Side Kick with Left

Side Kick with Right

Hook

Outer edge kick

Round house kick

Thrust kick

Back kick

Back kick

Jumping Round house kick

Jumping side kick with Right leg

Jumping side kick with Left leg

SPEED KICKING ON PAD WITH TIEING TUBE

Down heel kick with tube

Inner edge kick with tube

Outer edge kick with tube

Front thrust kick with tube

Round house kick with tube

Side kick with tube

Back kick with tube

Hook kick with tube

Jumping Round house kick with tube

Jumping Back kick with tube

Jumping side kick with tube

Jumping thrust kick with tube

Turning Jumping Round house
kick with tube Pic -A1

Turning Jumping Round house
kick with tube pic-A2

Turning Jumping Round house kick
with tube Pic -A3

WEDNESDAY: SPEED TRAINING OF PUNCHES

1st week schedule

(i) Knuckle pushups, Close fist and keep knuckle on ground with shoulder width distance and go down and come up. Do 5 push ups and 50 punches in 1 minute. See pictures A and B and C.

Pic - A

Pic- C

Pic - B

(ii) Single hand knuckle pushups: Do one hand knuckle pushups 5 times one hand 20 punches in 30 seconds and Change knuckles. Do alternate hands Do 2 sets. See picture A

Pic - A

(iii) Power pushups for speed & power punches

Sit on kneeling position with palms facing ground and jump forward onto your palms on the floor as shown in pictures A and B. and Do 3sets and get up and Do 60 punches in 1 minutes.

Pic -A

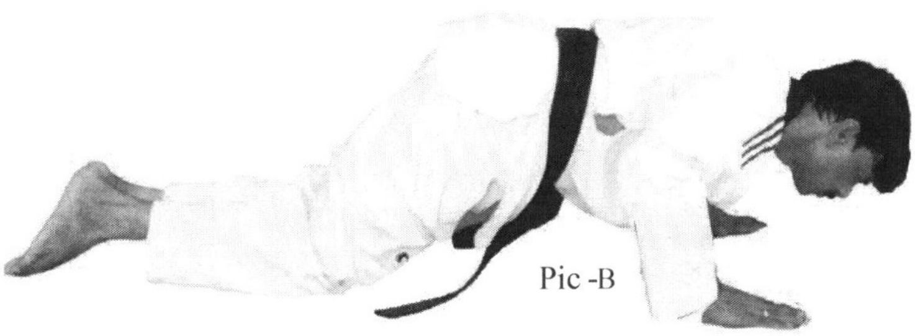

Pic -B

(iv) Pushing the kit bag and speed punch exercise: pushing the kit bag and 2 hands punches alternatively .Do 10 sets See pic- P1, P2 and P3

Pic –P1

Pic –P2

Pic –P3

Saturday: Tube kicking with single leg

1st week schedule

Tube kicking with single leg 15 kicks in 20 seconds one minute Rest between each single leg kicks

Do all kicks 15 times in 20 seconds each leg. Below mention kicks.

Side Kick with Left

Side Kick with Right

Hook

Outer edge kick

Round house kick

Thrust kick

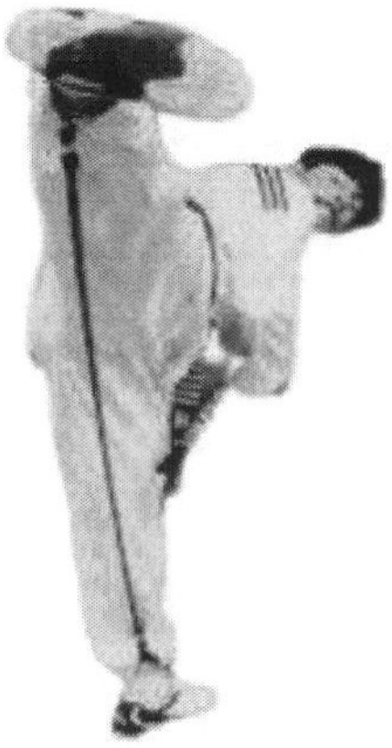

Back kick

Back kick

Jumping Round house kick

SPEED UNDER WATER KICKS & UNDER WATER PUNCHES

Sunday 1st week schedule, water workout (water must be chest level)

I. Under water kicks Do 1 to 8 kicks each leg 5 kicks (total 10 kicks).

1.Inner edge kick

2.Thrust kick

3.Side kick

4.Spinning kick

5.Round house kick

6. Hook kick

7. Outer edge kick

8. Hook kick and side kick with holding wall

II. a. Running in the water :

Running in the water 10 meters

b. Side Running in the water :

Running in the water right side 10 meters and left side 10 meters

c. knee raising in the water :

Knee raising in the water each leg 20 times (Total 40 times)

d. punches in the water :

(i)40 double punches in the water with alternative hands

(ii)40 single hands punches with the left hand and right hand (Total 80 punches)

e. check the speed of every individual kicks in 1 minute and make a of table improvement (minimum kicks must be 60 kicks in 1 minute)

f. check the speed of every individual kicks in 1 minute and make a of table improvement

<u>**SQUATS KICKS**</u>

Sunday Body Weight Squats Kicks below following kicks

1st week schedule

Sit on squat and get up and kick Down heel kick with one squat 3 kicks the Right leg and left leg and sit. Do 3 kicks each leg (i.e. Total 6 kicks) See pic-L1,pic-L2,pic-L3 and pic-4

Pic-L1

Pic-L2

Pic-L3

Pic-L4

Sit on squat and get up and kick inner edge with Right leg and left leg and sit. Do 3kicks each leg (i.e. Total 6 kicks) see pic- L5 and pic-L6.

Sit on squat and get up and kick outer edge with left leg and Right leg and sit. Do 3 kicks each leg (i.e. Total 6 kicks) See pic- L7 and pic-L8.

Sit on squat and get up and kick front thrust kick with Right leg and with the Left leg and sit. Do 3 kicks each leg (i.e. Total 6 kicks) See pic-L9 and pic-L10

Pic-L5

Pic-L6

Pic-L7

Pic-L8

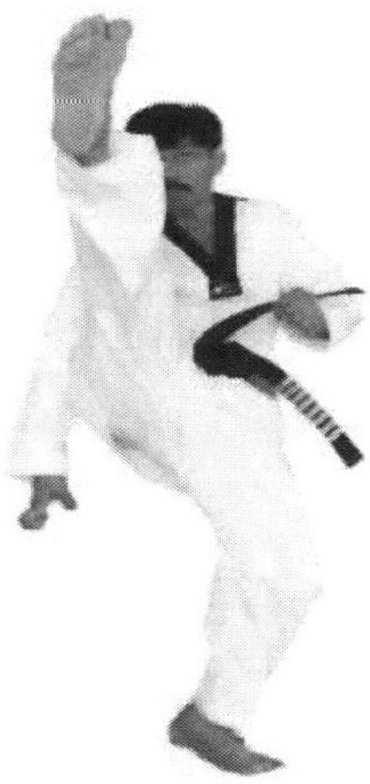

Pic-L9

Pic-L10

Sit on squat and get up and kick side kick with Right leg and with the Left leg and sit. Do 3 kicks each leg (i.e. Total 6 kicks) See pic-L11 and pic-L12.

Sit on squat and get up and kick front side kick with Right leg and with the Left leg and sit. Do 3 kicks each leg (i.e. Total 6 kicks) See pic-L13 and pic-L14.

Sit on squat and get up and kick Round house kick with Left leg and with the Right leg and sit. Do 3 kicks each leg (i.e. Total 6 kicks) See pic-L15 and pic-L16.

Pic-L11

Pic-L12

Pic-L13

Pic-L14

Pic-L15

Pic-L16 (side view)

Sit on squat and get up and kick Back kick with Right leg and with the Left leg and sit. Do 3 kicks each leg (i.e. Total 6 kicks) See pic-L17,pic-L18 and L19 Back kick in Front View.

Pic-L17

Pic-L18

Back kick Front view Pic-L19

Sit on squat and get up and kick Hook kick with Left leg and with the Right leg and sit. Do 3 kicks each leg (i.e. Total 6 kicks) See pic-L20,pic-L21 Front view.

Pic-L20 (Side View)

Hook kick front viewPic-L21

SPEED TRAINING OF KICKS-13 TO 15 YEARS

Monday –I 1st week schedule

½ kg ANKLE (LEG) WEIGHTS KICKS(Alternative Legs)

Wear a Ankle weight to your leg 1/2 kg each leg and start kicking all the kicks as shown in the pictures below. Each kick you need to do a minimum of 40 kicks each leg in 1 minute Rest for 2 minute. Do all 1 to 10 kicks.

1. down heel kick, alternative legs
2. Side Kick, alternative Legs
3. Spinning cart wheel kick, alternative legs
4. Hook Kick, alternative Legs
5. Trust Kick alternative Leg
6. Inner edge kicks alternative legs
7. Front side kicks alternative legs
8. Round House Kick Alternative Legs
9. Outer Edge Kick Alternative Legs
10. Back Kick and Do Alternative Leg

II. ½ kgs of Ankle Weight kick Controlling:

Do only 4 Kicks i.e., (1) Thrust Kick (2) Side Kick (3) Round House Kick (4) Back Kick

Control Each Leg at hips minimum do control for 25 seconds without any support.

III. Sitting kicks with ½ kg Ankle Weight:

Do only 4 kicks (1) snap kicks (2) Side kick (3) Round house kick (4) Hook kick.
Do each kick 70 times alternative legs Lie down on back and wear 1kgs Ankle weight and kick continuously snap kicks for 70 kicks

Kneel Led down and sit and hands support on the ground and raise your Right leg Right side and kick side kick continuously 30 kicks with wearing 1kg Ankle weights and change the leg and do with other leg same.

Kneel Led down and sit and hands support on the ground and kick round house kick sideways 30 times each leg with wearing 1kgs Ankle weight.

Kneel Led down and sit and hands support on the ground and kick Hook kick sideways 30 times each leg wearing 1kg Ankle weight

SPEED TRAINING OF PUNCHES - 13 TO 15 YEARS

Monday –I 1st week schedule

300 grams HAND WEIGHTS (Alternative Hands)

(a) Horse stand and hold 300grams hand weight and Do 60 punches with alternative hands in 1 minute

(b) Stand in front forward stance and punch with single Right hand over the left open hand (Bend at elbow in the front) 20 punches with Single hand with 300 grams hand weight in 1 minute
And change the hand i.e. change to left hand and punch with the same as Right hand punch.

(c) Speed sitting hand weights punches Sit on chair or stool and punch at least 40 times with alternative hand (with left hand and right hand)
Variation: your can do this sitting punches by blind folded i.e. with closing eyes, by imagining you are smashing with punch.

(d) Forearm Exercise
Forearm and wrist strengthening
Stand with holding one sided dumbbell 5 pounds (approximately) sideways should be besides you and pull up as high as possible, Front side. Do with left hand and with right hand. This exercise will strengthen wrist, forearm.

(e) Forearm Strengthening Exercise
Stand with holding one sided dumbbell 5 pounds (approximately) with right hand beside your thigh and pull up and down back side 12 times each hand alternately.

(f) Wrist Strengthening Exercises
Sit on chair and hold one side dumbbell 5 pounds (approximately) with Right forearm on the thighs and twist to left and right side with maximum strain. Do with other hand, Do 10 times each.

g) Forearm Strengthening
Sit on stool and holding bar with 10 pounds (approximately) weight with palm facing sky, as shown in picture with hands 10" inches apart and pull up your wrist to you and pull down 12 times. Note: Keep forearm and elbow on the thighs to balance the weight

(h) Forearm strengthening
Sit on stool and holding bar10 pounds (approximately) as shown in picture with hands 10" inches apart and pull to you and pull down 10 times. Note: Keep forearm and elbow on the thighs to balance the weight with palm facing floor in punching position

(i)Forearm Strengthening Exercises
Holding 12" to 15" long rod 5 pounds (approximately) tightly on the right side and twist 180 degrees for 20 times and change the hand and continue.
Variations: You can hold 2 rods either side of each hand and twist them.

(j)Forearm Strengthening
Hold 12" to 14" rod 5 pounds (approximately) in front of you and twist left and right 180 degrees angle with left hand 18 repetitions and change to right hand and do the same repetitions.

(k) Triceps Strengthening Exercise
Keep index and thumb of each hand join together and go for pushups with leg stretch out without bending knees. Do this exercise for 10 times daily.

Friday: Same as on Monday Schedule

SPEED PEDDLE KICKS(kicking on pad)

Tuesday 1st week schedule

I. PAD KICKING EACH LEG 20 KICKS 1 TO 15 KICKS

(1) Push kick

(2) Front thrust kick

(3) Side kick

(4) Round house kick

(5) Back kick

(6) Outer edge kick

(7) Inner edge kick

(8) Down heel kick

(9) Hook kick

(10) Jumping side kick

(11) Jumping Round house kick

(12) Jumping Back kick

(13) Spin kick

(14) Jumping spin kick

(15) Scissor kick

II. PAD KICKING LEFT LEG 20 KICKS IN 30 SECONDS SINGLE LEG

III. PAD KICKING RIGHT LEG 20 KICKS IN 30 SECONDS SINGLE LEG

Note: I,II and III Rest for 1 ½ minutes of each kick, Do all kicks accordingly

Thursday: Same as on Tuesday Schedule

SPEED NYLON / TUBE KICKING

Wednesday 1st week schedule

Speed Kicking With Tube

Tie bicycle tube or nylon thread and tie to your ankle and kick all kicks 20 times in 45 seconds alternative leg. Rest for 1 minute with each kick in air or kicking pad.
Do all kicks below mentioned stationary kicks 22 kicks in 45 seconds and 10 jumping kicks in 50 seconds.

Speed Kicking With Tube

Tie bicycle tube or nylon thread and tie to your ankle and kick all kicks 22 times with each leg. This improves kicking speed. Once in a week you can do single leg kick and alternative leg kicks. Do below mentioned kicks.

1. Side Kick with Left and Right Leg
2. Outer edge kick with Left and Right Leg
3. Inner edge kick with Left and Right Leg
4. Thrust kick with Left and Right Leg
5. Back kick with Left and Right Leg
6. Round house kick with Left and Right Leg
7. Hook Kick with Left and Right Leg
8. Jumping Round house kick with Left and Right Leg
9. Jumping side kick with Left and Right Leg
10. Down heel kick with Left and Right Leg
11. Jumping Thrust kick with Left and Right Leg
12. Jumping Back kick with Left and Right Leg

WEDNESDAY: <u>SPEED TRAINING OF PUNCHES</u>

1st week schedule

(i) Knuckle pushups, Close fist and keep knuckle on ground with shoulder width distance and go down and come up. Do 15 push ups and 60 punches in 1 minute.

(ii) Single hand knuckle pushups: Do one hand knuckle pushups 10 times one hand 20 punches in 1 minute and Change knuckles. Do alternate hands Do 2 sets

(iii) Power pushups for speed & power punches
Sit on kneeling position with palms facing ground and jump forward onto your palms on the Floor and Do 3 sets and get up and Do 125 punches in 2 minutes.

(iv) Pushing the kit bag and speed punch exercise: pushing the kit bag and 2 hands punches alternatively .Do 20 sets

Saturday: Tube kicking with single leg

1st week schedule

Tube kicking with single leg 20 kicks in 45 seconds one minute or 2 minutes Rest between each single leg kicks

Do all kicks 20 times in 45 seconds each leg. Below mentioned kicks.

1. Side Kick with Left and Right Leg
2. Hook Kick with Left and Right Leg
3. Outer edge kick with Left and Right Leg
4. Round house kick with Left and Right Leg
5. *Thrust kick* with Left and Right Leg
6. Back kick with Left and Right Leg
7. Jumping Round house kick with Left and Right Leg
8. Inner edge kick with Left and Right Leg

SPEED UNDER WATER KICKS & UNDER WATER PUNCHES

Sunday 1st week schedule, water workout (water must be chest level)

II. Under water kicks Do 1 to 8 kicks each leg 10 kicks (total 20 kicks)
Do below mentioned kicks

1.Inner edge kick

2.Thrust kick

3.Side kick

4.Spinning kick

5.Round house kick

6. Hook kick

7. Outer edge kick

8. Hook kick and side kick with holding wall

II. a. Running in the water :
Running in the water 15 meters

b. Side Running in the water :
Running in the water right side 15 meters and left side 15 meters

c. knee raising in the water :
Knee raising in the water each leg 30 times (Total 60 times)

d. punches in the water :
(i)90 double punches in the water with alternative hands
(ii)60 single hands punches with the left hand and right hand (Total 120 punches)

e. check the speed of every individual kicks in 1 minute and make a table of improvement (minimum kicks must be 140 kicks in 1 minute in Air every week)

<u>SQUATS KICKS</u>

Sunday Body Weight Squats Kicks below following kicks

1st week schedule

Sit on squat and get up and kick Down heel kick with one squat 2 kicks with the Right leg and left leg and sit. Do 8 kicks each leg (i.e. Total 16 kicks)

Sit on squat and get up and kick inner edge with Right leg and left leg and sit. Do 8 kicks each leg (i.e. Total 16kicks).

Sit on squat and get up and kick outer edge with left leg and Right leg and sit. Do 8 kicks each leg (i.e. Total 16 kicks).

Sit on squat and get up and kick front thrust kick with Right leg and with the Left leg and sit. Do 8 kicks each leg (i.e. Total 16 kicks) .

Sit on squat and get up and kick side kick with Right leg and with the Left leg and sit. Do 8 kicks each leg (i.e. Total 16 kicks).

Sit on squat and get up and kick front side kick with Right leg and with the Left leg and sit. Do 8 kicks each leg (i.e. Total 16 kicks).

Sit on squat and get up and kick Round house kick with Left leg and with the Right leg and sit. Do 8 kicks each leg (i.e. Total 16 kicks).

Sit on squat and get up and kick Back kick with Right leg and with the Left leg and sit. Do 8 kicks each leg (i.e. Total 16 kicks).

Sit on squat and get up and kick Hook kick with Left leg and with the Right leg and sit. Do 8 kicks each leg (i.e. Total 16 kicks).

SPEED TRAINING OF KICKS - BELOW 13 YEARS

Monday – 1st week schedule

50 KICKS IN 2 MINITUES

Each kick you need to do a minimum of 25kicks each leg in 1 minute Rest for 2 minute. Do all 1 to 10 kicks. Below mention kicks

1. down heel kick, alternative legs
2. Side Kick, alternative Legs
3. Spinning cart wheel kick, alternative legs
4. Hook Kick, alternative Legs
5. Trust Kick alternative Leg
6. Inner edge kicks alternative legs
7. Front side kicks alternative legs
8. Round House Kick Alternative Legs
9. Outer Edge Kick Alternative Legs
10. Back Kick and Do Alternative Leg

II. Kick Controlling:

Do only 4 Kicks i.e., (1) Thrust Kick (2) Side Kick (3) Round House Kick (4) Back Kick

Control Each Leg at hips minimum do control for 15 to 20 seconds without any support.

III. Sitting kicks:

Do only 4 kicks (1) snap kicks (2) Side kick (3) Round house kick (4) Hook kick.
Do each kick 35 times alternative legs Lie down on back and kick continuously snap kicks start from 25 kicks to 35 kicks

Kneel Led down and sit and hands support on the ground and raise your Right leg Right side and kick side kick continuously 25 to 35 and change the leg and do with other leg same.

Kneel down and sit and hands support on the ground and kick round house kick sideways 25 to 35 times each leg.

Kneel down and sit and hands support on the ground and kick Hook kick sideways 25 to 35 times each leg.

SPEED TRAINING OF PUNCHES - BELOW 13 YEARS

Monday –I 1st week schedule

100 punches in 1 minute (Alternative Hands)

(a) Horse stand and Do 100 punches with alternative hands in 1 minute Do 2 sets.

(b) Stand in front forward stance and punch with single Right hand over the left open hand (Bend at elbow in the front) 40 punches with Single hand with in 1 minute Do 2 sets And change the hand i.e. change to left hand and punch with the same as Right hand punch.

(c) Speed sitting hand punches Sit on chair or stool and punch at least 50 times with alternative hand (with left hand and right hand) Do 2 sets.
Variation: your can do this sitting punches by blind folded i.e. with closing eyes, by imagining you are smashing with punch.

(d) Punches on x-ray film: you can practices 40 with each hand (total 80 punches)

(e) Triceps Strengthening Exercise
Keep index and thumb of each hand join together and go for pushups with leg stretch out without bending knees. Do this exercise for 6 to 8 times daily.

Friday: Same as on Monday Schedule

SPEED PEDDLE KICKS(kicking on pad)

Tuesday 1st week schedule

I. PAD KICKING EACH LEG 15 KICKS 1 TO 15 KICKS

(1) Push kick - 15 kicks each leg
(2) Front thrust kick " "
(3) Side kick " "
(4) Round house kick " "
(5) Back kick " "
(6) Outer edge kick " "
(7) Inner edge kick " "
(8) Down heel kick " "
(9) Hook kick " "
(10) Jumping side kick " "
(11) Jumping Round house kick " "

(12) Jumping Back kick - 8 kicks each leg

(13) Spin kick - 15 kicks each leg

(14) Jumping spin kick - 8 kicks each leg

(15) Scissor kick - 15 kicks each leg

II. PAD KICKING LEFT LEG 15 KICKS IN 30 SECONDS SINGLE LEG

III. PAD KICKING RIGHT LEG 15 KICKS IN 30 SECONDS SINGLE LEG

Note: I,II and III Rest for 1 minute of each kick, Do all kicks accordingly

Thursday: Same as on Tuesday Schedule

WEDNESDAY: <u>SPEED TRAINING OF PUNCHES</u>

1st week schedule

(i) Knuckle pushups, Close fist and keep knuckle on ground with shoulder width distance and go down and come up or palms pushups Do 8 pushups and 40 punches in 1 minute.

(ii) Single hand knuckle or palms pushups: Do one hand knuckle pushups 8 times one hand 20 punches in 1 minute and Change knuckles. Do alternate hands Do 2 sets

(iii) Power pushups for speed & power punches
Sit on kneeling position with palms facing ground and jump forward onto your palms on the Floor and Do 3 sets and get up and Do 100 punches in 2 minutes.

(iv) Pushing the kit bag and speed punch exercise: pushing the kit bag and 2 hands punches alternatively .Do 15 sets

SUNDAY 1ST WEEK SCHEDULE, WATER WORKOUT (WATER MUST BE CHEST LEVEL)

I. a. Running in the water :
Running in the water 10 meters

b. Side Running in the water :
Running in the water right side 10 meters and left side 10 meters

c. knee raising in the water :
Knee raising in the water each leg 25 times (Total 50 times)

d. check every week the speed of every individual kicks in 1 minute and make a table of improvement (minimum kicks must be 100 kicks in 1 minute in Air every week)

2nd Week

Speed Training schedule for 15 Years and above

Speed Training schedule for 13 – 15 Years

Speed Training schedule for below 13 years

"Every success of achievement or failure is not a history, but every history is always failure achievement in any field"

- Grand Master M. Jayanth Reddy

SPEED TRAINING OF KICKS- 15 YEARS AND ABOVE

Monday –I 2nd week schedule

1kg ANKLE (LEG) WEIGHTS KICKS(Alternative Legs)

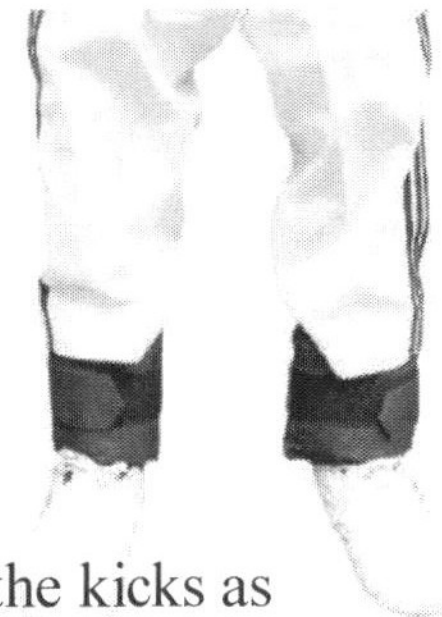

Wear a Ankle weight to your leg 1 kg each leg and start kicking all the kicks as shown in the pictures below. Each kick you need to do a minimum of 8 kicks each leg Rest for 1 minute. Do all 1 to 10 kicks.

1.DOWN HEEL KICK, ALTERNATIVE LEGS

2.SIDE KICK, ALTERNATIVE LEGS

3.SPINNING CART WHEEL KICK, ALTERNATIVE LEGS

4.HOOK KICK, ALTERNATIVE LEGS

5.TRUST KICK ALTENATIVE LEG

6. INNER EDGE KICKS ALTERNATIVE LEGS

7. FRONT SIDE KICKS ALTERNATIVE LEGS

8. ROUND HOUSE KICK ALTERNATIVE LEGS

9. OUTER EDGE KICK ALTERNATIVE LEGS

10. BACK KICK AND DO ALTERNATIVE LEG

II. 1kgs of Ankle Weight kick Controlling:

Do only 4 Kicks i.e., (1) Thrust Kick (2) Side Kick (3) Round House Kick (4) Back Kick Control Each Leg at hips minimum do control for 10 to 15 seconds without any support. See Picture A,B,C and D. Do 2 sets each.

Pic-A
Thrust Kick, Alternative Legs

Pic-B
Side Kick, Alternative Legs

Pic-C
Round House Kick Alternative Legs

Pic-D

Back Kick do with Alternative Leg

III. Sitting kicks with 1 kgs Ankle weight:

Do only 4 kicks (1) snap kicks (2) Side kick (3) Round house kick (4) Hook kick. Do each kick 50 times alternative legs Lie down on back and wear 1 kgs Ankle weight and kick continuously snap kicks for 25 to 30 kicks see pic-P1 ,pic- P2 and p3.

Pic-P1

Pic-P2

Pic-P3

Kneel led down and sit and hands support on the ground and raise your Right leg Right side and kick side kick continuously 25 to 30 kicks with wearing 1kg Ankle weights and change the leg and do with other leg same. See pic-P4 and pic-P5.

pic-P4

pic-P5

Kneel led down and sit and hands support on the ground and kick round house kick sideways 25 to 30 times each leg with wearing 1kgs Ankle weight. See pic-P6 and pic-P7

pic-P6

pic-P7

Kneel led down ana sit ana nanas support on the ground and kick Hook kick sideways 25 to 30 times each leg wearing 1kgs Ankle weight. See pic-P8 and pic-P9.

pic-P8

pic-P9

SPEED TRAINING OF PUNCHES - 15 YEARS AND ABOVE

Monday –I 2nd week schedule

1kgs HAND WEIGHTS (Alternative Hands)

(a) Horse stand Horse stand and hold 1 kg hand weight and Do 60 punches with alternative hands with 1kg hand weight in 1 minute See picture 1 and 2

Pic -1

Pic -2

(b) Stand in front forward stance and punch with single Right hand over the left open hand (Bend at elbow in the front) 25 punches with Single hand with 1kg hand weight in 1 minute And change the hand i.e. change to left hand and punch with the same as Right hand punch. See picture 3,4,5 and 6

(c) Speed sitting hand weights punches Sit on chair or stool and punch at least 50 times with alternative hand (with left hand and right hand)

Variation: your can do this sitting punches by blind folded i.e. with closing eyes, by imagining you are smashing with punch. See picture 7 and 8

Pic -7

Pic -8

Forearm Strengthening Exercises 1

Holding 12" to 15" long rod 3 pounds (approximately) tightly on the right side and twist 180degrees for 10 times and change the hand and continue. See pictures A, B, C

Variations: You can hold 2 rods either side of each hand and twist them.

Pic - A

Pic - B

Pic - C

Forearm Strengthening 2

Hold 12" to 14" rod 3 pounds (approximately) in front of you and twist left and right 180 degrees angle with left hand 10 times repetitions and change to right hand and do the same repetitions. See pictures A, B, C, D, E and F.

Pic - A

Pic – B

Pic – C

Pic- D

Pic – E

Pic - F

Triceps Strengthening Exercise 3
Keep index and thumb of each hand join together and go for pushups with leg stretch out without bending knees. Do this exercise for 8 times daily. See pictures A and B.

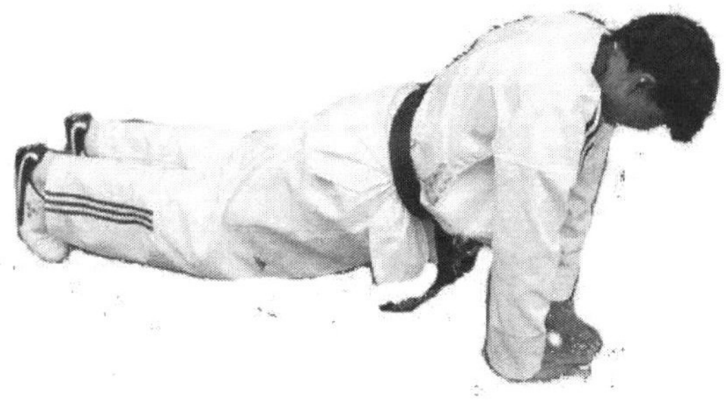

Pic A

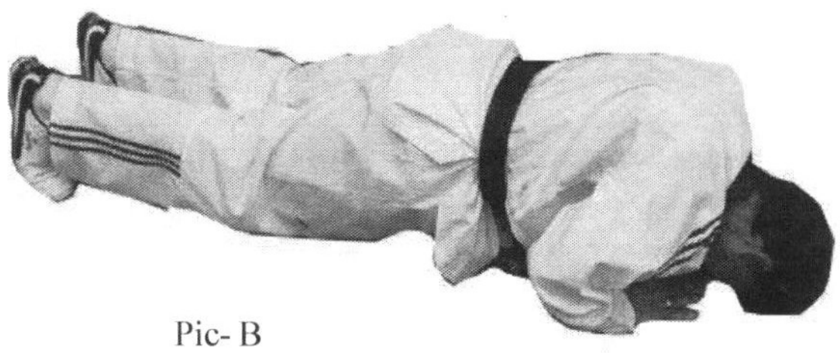

Pic- B

Friday: Same as on Monday Schedule

SPEED PEDDLE KICKS(kicking on pad)

Tuesday 2nd week schedule

I. PAD KICKING EACH LEG 15 KICKS 1 TO 15 KICKS

(1) Push kick
(2) Front thrust kick
(3) Side kick
(4) Round house kick
(5) Back kick
(6) Outer edge kick
(7) Inner edge kick
(8) Down heel kick
(9) Hook kick
(10) Jumping side kick
(11) Jumping Round house kick
(12) Jumping Back kick
(13) Spin kick
(14) Jumping spin kick
(15) Scissor kick

Jumping thrust kick

Push Kick on Pad -1

Front thrust kick on pad -2

Side kick on pad -3

Round house on pad-4

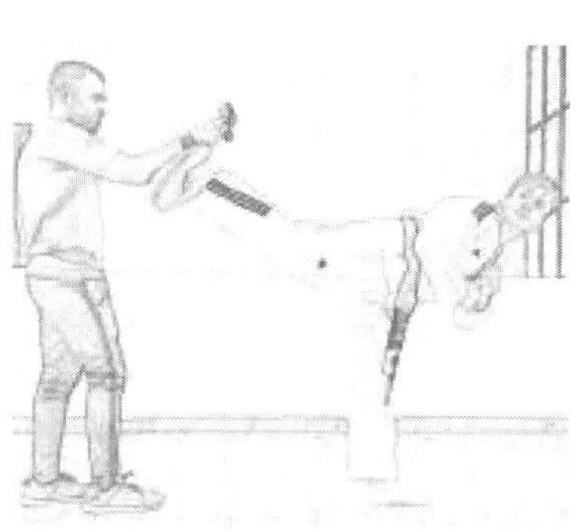

Back kick on pad – 5

Outer edge kick on pad – 6

Inner edge kick on pad -7

Down heel kick on pad -8

Hook kick on pad – 9

Jumping side kick on pad – 10

Jumping Round house kick on pad - 11

Jumping Back kick on pad – 12

Jumping spin kick on pad - 13

Front Side kick -14

Scissor kick-15

II. PAD KICKING LEFT LEG 15 KICKS IN 30 SECONDS SINGLE LEG

III. PAD KICKING RIGHT LEG 15 KICKS IN 30 SECONDS SINGLE LEG

Note: I,II and III Rest for 1 minutes of each kick, Do all kicks accordingly

Thursday: Same as on Tuesday Schedule

SPEED NYLON / TUBE KICKING

Wednesday 2nd week schedule

Speed Kicking With Tube

Tie bicycle tube or nylon thread and tie to your ankle and kick all kicks 15 times in 20 seconds alternative leg. Rest for 1 minute with each kick.
Do all kicks below mentioned stationary kicks 15 kicks in 20 seconds and 8 jumping kicks in 15 seconds.

Speed Kicking With Tube

Tie bicycle tube or nylon thread and tie to your ankle and kick all kicks 15 times with each leg. This improves kicking speed. Once in a week you can do single leg kick and alternative leg kicks.

Side Kick with Left

Side Kick with Right

Hook

Outer edge kick

Round house kick

Thrust kick

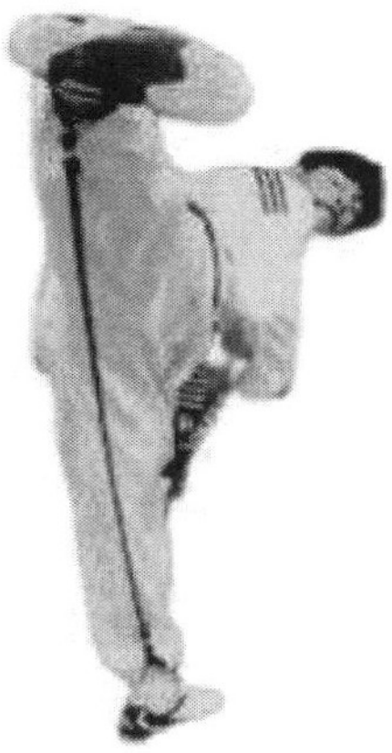

Back kick

Back kick

Jumping Round house kick

Jumping side kick with Right leg

Jumping side kick with Left leg

SPEED KICKING ON PAD WITH TIEING TUBE

Down heel kick with tube

Inner edge kick with tube

Outer edge kick with tube

Front thrust kick with tube

Round house kick with tube

Side kick with tube

Back kick with tube

Hook kick with tube

Jumping Round house kick with tube

Jumping Back kick with tube

Jumping side kick with tube

Jumping thrust kick with tube

Turning Jumping Round house
kick with tube Pic -A1

Turning Jumping Round house
kick with tube pic-A2

Turning Jumping Round house kick
with tube Pic -A3

WEDNESDAY: <u>SPEED TRAINING OF PUNCHES</u>

2nd week schedule

(ii) Knuckle pushups, Close fist and keep knuckle on ground with shoulder width distance and go down and come up. Do 10 push ups and 75 punches in 1 minute. See pictures A and B and C

Pic - A

Pic- C

Pic - B

(ii) Single hand knuckle pushups: Do one hand knuckle pushups 8 times one hand 25 punches in 1 minute and Change knuckles. Do alternate hands Do 2 sets. See picture A

Pic - A

(iii) Power pushups for speed & power punches

Sit on kneeling position with palms facing ground and jump forward onto your palms on the floor as shown in pictures A and B. Do 5 sets and get up and Do 75 punches in 1 minutes.

Pic A

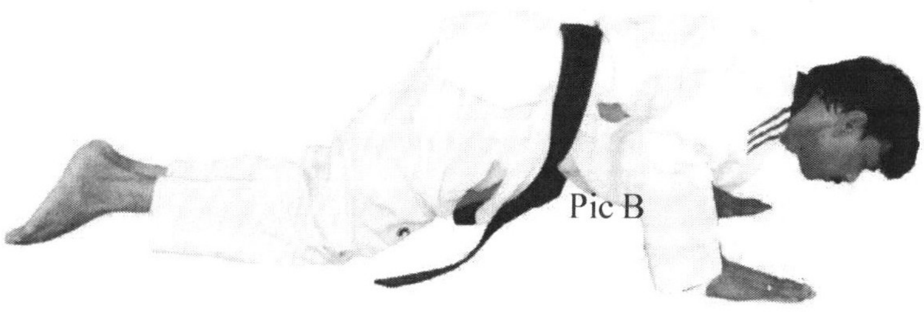

Pic B

(iv) Pushing the kit bag and speed punch exercise: pushing the kit bag and 2 hands punches alternatively .Do 15 sets See pic- P1, P2 and P3

Pic –P1

Pic –P2

Pic –P3

Saturday: Tube kicking with single leg

2nd week schedule

Tube kicking with single leg 20 kicks in 25 seconds one minute Rest between each single leg kicks

Do all kicks 20 times in 25 seconds each leg. Below mention kicks.

Side Kick with Left

Side Kick with Right

Hook

Outer edge kick

Round house kick

Thrust kick

Back kick

Back kick

Jumping Round house kick

SPEED UNDER WATER KICKS & UNDER WATER PUNCHES

Sunday 2nd week schedule, water workout (water must be chest level)

I. Under water kicks Do 1 to 8 kicks each leg 5 kicks (total 10 kicks) in 30 seconds.

1.Inner edge kick

2.Thrust kick

3.Side kick

4.Spinning kick

5.Round house kick

6. Hook kick

7. Outer edge kick

8. Hook kick and side kick with holding wall

III. **a. Running in the water :**

Running in the water 15 meters

b. Side Running in the water :

Running in the water right side 15 meters and left side 15 meters

c. knee raising in the water :

Knee raising in the water each leg 30 times (Total 60 times)

d. punches in the water :
(i)50 double punches in the water with alternative hands
(ii)50 single hands punches with the left hand and right hand (Total 100 punches)

e. check the speed of every individual kicks in 1 minute and make a of table improvement (minimum kicks must be 75 kicks in 1 minute)

f. check the speed of every individual kicks in 1 minute and make a of table improvement

SQUATS KICKS

Sunday Body Weight Squats Kicks below following kicks
2nd week schedule

Sit on squat and get up and kick down heel kick with one squat 2 kicks the Right leg and left leg and sit. Do 5 kicks each leg (i.e. Total 10 kicks) See pic-L1,pic-L2,pic-L3 and pic-4

Pic-L1

Pic-L2

Pic-L3

Pic-L4

Sit on squat and get up and kick inner edge with Right leg and left leg and sit. Do 5kicks each leg (i.e. Total 10 kicks) see pic- L5 and pic-L6.

Sit on squat and get up and kick outer edge with left leg and Right leg and sit. Do 5 kicks each leg (i.e. Total 10 kicks) See pic- L7 and pic-L8.

Sit on squat and get up and kick front thrust kick with Right leg and with the Left leg and sit. Do 5 kicks each leg (i.e. Total 10 kicks) See pic-L9 and pic-L10

Pic-L5

Pic-L6

Pic-L7

Pic-L8

Pic-L9

Pic-L10

Sit on squat and get up and kick side kick with Right leg and with the Left leg and sit. Do 5 kicks each leg (i.e. Total 10 kicks) See pic-L11 and pic-L12.

Sit on squat and get up and kick front side kick with Right leg and with the Left leg and sit. Do 5 kicks each leg (i.e. Total 10 kicks) See pic-L13 and pic-L14.

Sit on squat and get up and kick Round house kick with Left leg and with the Right leg and sit. Do 5 kicks each leg (i.e. Total 10 kicks) See pic-L15 and pic-L16.

Pic-L11

Pic-L12

Pic-

Pic-L14

Pic-L15

Pic-L16 (side view)

Sit on squat and get up and kick Back kick with Right leg and with the Left leg and sit. Do 5 kicks each leg (i.e. Total 10 kicks) See pic-L17,pic-L18 and L19 Back kick in Front View.

Pic-L17

Pic-L18

Back kick Front view Pic-L19

Sit on squat and get up and kick Hook kick with Left leg and with the Right leg and sit. Do 5 kicks each leg (i.e. Total 10 kicks) See pic-L20,pic-L21 Front view.

Pic-L20 (Side View)

Hook kick front viewPic-L21

SPEED TRAINING OF KICKS-13 TO 15 YEARS

Monday –I 2nd week schedule

½ kg ANKLE (LEG) WEIGHTS KICKS(Alternative Legs)

Wear a Ankle weight to your leg 1/2 kg each leg and start kicking all the kicks as shown in the pictures below. Each kick you need to do a minimum of 40 kicks each leg in 1 minute Rest for 2 minute. Do all 1 to 10 kicks.

1. down heel kick, alternative legs
2. Side Kick, alternative Legs
3. Spinning cart wheel kick, alternative legs
4. Hook Kick, alternative Legs
5. Trust Kick alternative Leg
6. Inner edge kicks alternative legs
7. Front side kicks alternative legs
8. Round House Kick Alternative Legs
9. Outer Edge Kick Alternative Legs
10. Back Kick and Do Alternative Leg

II. ½ kgs of Ankle Weight kick Controlling:

Do only 4 Kicks i.e., (1) Thrust Kick (2) Side Kick (3) Round House Kick (4) Back Kick

Control Each Leg at hips minimum do control for 25 seconds without any support.

III. Sitting kicks with ½ kg Ankle Weight:

Do only 4 kicks (1) snap kicks (2) Side kick (3) Round house kick (4) Hook kick.
Do each kick 70 times alternative legs Lie down on back and wear 1kgs Ankle weight and kick continuously snap kicks for 70 kicks

Kneel Led down and sit and hands support on the ground and raise your Right leg Right side and kick side kick continuously 30 kicks with wearing 1kg Ankle weights and change the leg and do with other leg same.

Kneel Led down and sit and hands support on the ground and kick round house kick sideways 30 times each leg with wearing 1kgs Ankle weight.

Kneel Led down and sit and hands support on the ground and kick Hook kick sideways 30 times each leg wearing 1kg Ankle weight

SPEED TRAINING OF PUNCHES - 13 TO 15 YEARS

Monday –I 2nd week schedule

300 grams HAND WEIGHTS (Alternative Hands)

(a) Horse stand and hold 300grams hand weight and Do 60 punches with alternative hands in 1 minute

(b) Stand in front forward stance and punch with single Right hand over the left open hand (Bend at elbow in the front) 20 punches with Single hand with 300 grams hand weight in 1 minute
And change the hand i.e. change to left hand and punch with the same as Right hand punch.

(c) Speed sitting hand weights punches Sit on chair or stool and punch at least 40 times with alternative hand (with left hand and right hand)
Variation: your can do this sitting punches by blind folded i.e. with closing eyes, by imagining you are smashing with punch.

(d) Forearm Exercise
Forearm and wrist strengthening
Stand with holding one sided dumbbell 5 pounds (approximately) sideways should be besides you and pull up as high as possible, Front side. Do with left hand and with right hand. This exercise will strengthen wrist, forearm.

(e) Forearm Strengthening Exercise
Stand with holding one sided dumbbell 5 pounds (approximately) with right hand beside your thigh and pull up and down back side 12 times each hand alternately.

(f) Wrist Strengthening Exercises
Sit on chair and hold one side dumbbell 5 pounds (approximately) with Right forearm on the thighs and twist to left and right side with maximum strain. Do with other hand, Do 10 times each.

g) Forearm Strengthening
Sit on stool and holding bar with 10 pounds (approximately) weight with palm facing sky, as shown in picture with hands 10" inches apart and pull up your wrist to you and pull down 12 times. Note: Keep forearm and elbow on the thighs to balance the weight

(h) Forearm strengthening
Sit on stool and holding bar10 pounds (approximately) as shown in picture with hands 10" inches apart and pull to you and pull down 10 times. Note: Keep forearm and elbow on the thighs to balance the weight with palm facing floor in punching position

(i)Forearm Strengthening Exercises
Holding 12" to 15" long rod 5 pounds (approximately) tightly on the right side and twist 180 degrees for 20 times and change the hand and continue.
Variations: You can hold 2 rods either side of each hand and twist them.

(j)Forearm Strengthening

Hold 12" to 14" rod 5 pounds (approximately) in front of you and twist left and right 180 degrees angle with left hand 18 repetitions and change to right hand and do the same repetitions.

(k) Triceps Strengthening Exercise

Keep index and thumb of each hand join together and go for pushups with leg stretch out without bending knees. Do this exercise for 10 times daily.

Friday: Same as on Monday Schedule

SPEED PEDDLE KICKS(kicking on pad)

Tuesday 2nd week schedule

I. PAD KICKING EACH LEG 20 KICKS 1 TO 15 KICKS

(1) Push kick

(2) Front thrust kick

(3) Side kick

(4) Round house kick

(5) Back kick

(6) Outer edge kick

(7) Inner edge kick

(8) Down heel kick

(9) Hook kick

(10) Jumping side kick

(11) Jumping Round house kick

(12) Jumping Back kick

(13) Spin kick

(14) Jumping spin kick

(15) Scissor kick

II. PAD KICKING LEFT LEG 20 KICKS IN 30 SECONDS SINGLE LEG

III. PAD KICKING RIGHT LEG 20 KICKS IN 30 SECONDS SINGLE LEG

Note: I,II and III Rest for 1 ½ minutes of each kick, Do all kicks accordingly

Thursday: Same as on Tuesday Schedule

SPEED NYLON / TUBE KICKING

Wednesday 2nd week schedule

Speed Kicking With Tube

Tie bicycle tube or nylon thread and tie to your ankle and kick all kicks 20 times in 45 seconds alternative leg. Rest for 1 minute with each kick in air or kicking pad.
Do all kicks below mentioned stationary kicks 22 kicks in 45 seconds and 10 jumping kicks in 50 seconds.

Speed Kicking With Tube

Tie bicycle tube or nylon thread and tie to your ankle and kick all kicks 22 times with each leg.

This improves kicking speed. Once in a week you can do single leg kick and alternative leg kicks.

Do below mentioned kicks.

1. Side Kick with Left and Right Leg
2. Outer edge kick with Left and Right Leg
3. Inner edge kick with Left and Right Leg
4. Thrust kick with Left and Right Leg
5. Back kick with Left and Right Leg
6. Round house kick with Left and Right Leg
7. Hook Kick with Left and Right Leg
8. Jumping Round house kick with Left and Right Leg
9. Jumping side kick with Left and Right Leg
10. Down heel kick with Left and Right Leg
11. Jumping Thrust kick with Left and Right Leg
12. Jumping Back kick with Left and Right Leg

WEDNESDAY: **SPEED TRAINING OF PUNCHES**

2nd week schedule

(i) Knuckle pushups, Close fist and keep knuckle on ground with shoulder width distance and go down and come up. Do 15 push ups and 60 punches in 1 minute.

(ii) Single hand knuckle pushups: Do one hand knuckle pushups 10 times one hand 20 punches in 1 minute and Change knuckles. Do alternate hands Do 2 sets

(iii) Power pushups for speed & power punches
Sit on kneeling position with palms facing ground and jump forward onto your palms on the Floor and Do 3 sets and get up and Do 125 punches in 2 minutes.

(iv) Pushing the kit bag and speed punch exercise: pushing the kit bag and 2 hands punches alternatively .Do 20 sets

Saturday: Tube kicking with single leg

2nd week schedule

Tube kicking with single leg 20 kicks in 45 seconds one minute or 2 minutes Rest between each single leg kicks

Do all kicks 20 times in 45 seconds each leg. Below mentioned kicks.

1. Side Kick with Left and Right Leg
2. Hook Kick with Left and Right Leg
3. Outer edge kick with Left and Right Leg
4. Round house kick with Left and Right Leg
5. *Thrust kick* with Left and Right Leg
6. Back kick with Left and Right Leg
7. Jumping Round house kick with Left and Right Leg
8. Inner edge kick with Left and Right Leg

SPEED UNDER WATER KICKS & UNDER WATER PUNCHES

Sunday 2nd week schedule, water workout (water must be chest level)

I. Under water kicks Do 1 to 8 kicks each leg 10 kicks (total 20 kicks)
Do below mentioned kicks

1.Inner edge kick

2.Thrust kick

3.Side kick

4.Spinning kick

5.Round house kick

6. Hook kick

7. Outer edge kick

8. Hook kick and side kick with holding wall

II. a. Running in the water :
Running in the water 15 meters

b. Side Running in the water :
Running in the water right side 15 meters and left side 15 meters

c. knee raising in the water :
Knee raising in the water each leg 30 times (Total 60 times)

d. punches in the water :
(i)90 double punches in the water with alternative hands
(ii)60 single hands punches with the left hand and right hand (Total 120 punches)

e. check the speed of every individual kicks in 1 minute and make a table of improvement (minimum kicks must be 140 kicks in 1 minute in Air every week)

SQUATS KICKS

Sunday Body Weight Squats Kicks below following kicks 2nd week schedule

Sit on squat and get up and kick Down heel kick with one squat 2 kicks with the Right leg and left leg and sit. Do 8 kicks each leg (i.e. Total 16 kicks)

Sit on squat and get up and kick inner edge with Right leg and left leg and sit. Do 8 kicks each leg (i.e. Total 16kicks).

Sit on squat and get up and kick outer edge with left leg and Right leg and sit. Do 8 kicks each leg (i.e. Total 16 kicks).

Sit on squat and get up and kick front thrust kick with Right leg and with the Left leg and sit. Do 8 kicks each leg (i.e. Total 16 kicks).

Sit on squat and get up and kick side kick with Right leg and with the Left leg and sit. Do 8 kicks each leg (i.e. Total 16 kicks).

Sit on squat and get up and kick front side kick with Right leg and with the Left leg and sit. Do 8 kicks each leg (i.e. Total 16 kicks).

Sit on squat and get up and kick Round house kick with Left leg and with the Right leg and sit. Do 8 kicks each leg (i.e. Total 16 kicks).

Sit on squat and get up and kick back kick with Right leg and with the Left leg and sit. Do 8 kicks each leg (i.e. Total 16 kicks).

Sit on squat and get up and kick Hook kick with Left leg and with the Right leg and sit. Do 8 kicks each leg (i.e. Total 16 kicks).

SPEED TRAINING OF KICKS - BELOW 13 YEARS

Monday –I 2nd & 3rd week schedule

70 KICKS IN 2 MINITUES

Each kick you need to do a minimum of 35 kicks each leg in 1 minute Rest for 2 minute. Do all 1 to 10 kicks. Below mention kicks

1. down heel kick, alternative legs
2. Side Kick, alternative Legs
3. Spinning cart wheel kick, alternative legs
4. Hook Kick, alternative Legs
5. Trust Kick alternative Leg
6. Inner edge kicks alternative legs
7. Front side kicks alternative legs
8. Round House Kick Alternative Legs
9. Outer Edge Kick Alternative Legs
10. Back Kick and Do Alternative Leg

II. Kick Controlling:

Do only 4 Kicks i.e., (1) Thrust Kick (2) Side Kick (3) Round House Kick (4) Back Kick

Control Each Leg at hips minimum do control for 20 to 25 seconds without any support.

III. Sitting kicks:

Do only 4 kicks (1) snap kicks (2) Side kick (3) Round house kick (4) Hook kick.
Do each kick 50 times alternative legs Lie down on back and kick continuously snap kicks start from 25 kicks to 50 kicks

Kneel Led down and sit and hands support on the ground and raise your Right leg Right side and kick side kick continuously 25 to 50 and change the leg and do with other leg same.

Kneel down and sit and hands support on the ground and kick round house kick sideways 25 to 50 times each leg.

Kneel down and sit and hands support on the ground and kick Hook kick sideways 25 to 50 times each leg.

Variation: kicks on x-ray film. You can do all kicks and all punches on x-ray film each kick 10 times and 40 punch with 2 hands.

SPEED TRAINING OF PUNCHES - BELOW 13 YEARS

Monday –I 2nd & 3rd week schedule

120 punches in 1 minute (Alternative Hands)

a) Horse stand and Do 120 punches with alternative hands in 1 minute Do 2 sets.

(b) Stand in front forward stance and punch with single Right hand over the left open hand (Bend at elbow in the front) 60 punches with Single hand with in 1 minute Do 2 sets And change the hand i.e. change to left hand and punch with the same as Right hand punch.

(c) Speed sitting hand punches Sit on chair or stool and punch at least 80 times with alternative hand (with left hand and right hand) Do 2 sets.
Variation: your can do this sitting punches by blind folded i.e. with closing eyes, by imagining you are smashing with punch.

(d) Punches on x-ray film: you can practices 60 with each hand (total 120 punches)

(e) Triceps Strengthening Exercise
Keep index and thumb of each hand join together and go for pushups with leg stretch out without bending knees. Do this exercise for 8 to 10 times daily.

Friday: Same as on Monday Schedule

SPEED PEDDLE KICKS(kicking on pad)

Tuesday 2nd &3rd week schedule

I. PAD KICKING EACH LEG 20 KICKS 1 TO 15 KICKS

(1) Push kick - 20 kicks each leg
(2) Front thrust kick " "
(3) Side kick " "
(4) Round house kick " "
(5) Back kick " "
(6) Outer edge kick " "
(7) Inner edge kick " "
(8) Down heel kick " "
(9) Hook kick " "
(10) Jumping side kick " "
(11) Jumping Round house kick " "

(12) Jumping Back kick - 12 kicks each leg

(13) Spin kick -20 kicks each leg

(14) Jumping spin kick -12 kicks each leg

(15) Scissor kick - 20 kicks each leg

II. PAD KICKING LEFT LEG 20 KICKS IN 1MINITE SINGLE LEG

III. PAD KICKING RIGHT LEG 20 KICKS IN 1MINITE SINGLE LEG

Note: I,II and III Rest for 1 ½ minutes of each kick, Do all kicks accordingly

Thursday: Same as on Tuesday Schedule

WEDNESDAY: SPEED TRAINING OF PUNCHES

2nd & 3rd week schedule

(i) Knuckle pushups, Close fist and keep knuckle on ground with shoulder width distance and go down and come up or palms pushups Do 10 pushups and 50 punches in 1 minute.

(ii) Single hand knuckle or palms pushups: Do one hand knuckle pushups 10 times one hand 30 punches in 1 minute and Change knuckles. Do alternate hands Do 2 sets

(iii) Power pushups for speed & power punches
Sit on kneeling position with palms facing ground and jump forward onto your palms on the Floor and Do 3 sets and get up and Do 125 punches in 2 minutes.

(iv) Pushing the kit bag and speed punch exercise: pushing the kit bag and 2 hands punches alternatively .Do 20 sets

SPEED UNDER WATER KICKS & UNDER WATER PUNCHES

Sunday 2nd & 3rd week schedule, water workout (water must be chest level)

I. Under water kicks Do 1 to 8 kicks each leg 8 kicks (total 16 kicks) in 1 minute
Do below mentioned kicks

1.Inner edge kick

2.Thrust kick

3.Side kick

4.Spinning kick

5.Round house kick

6. Hook kick

7. Outer edge kick

8. Hook kick and side kick with holding wall

II. a. Running in the water :
Running in the water 10 meters

b. Side Running in the water :
Running in the water right side 10 meters and left side 10 meters

c. knee raising in the water :
Knee raising in the water each leg 25 times (Total 50 times)

d. punches in the water :
(i) 50 double punches in the water with alternative hands
(ii)40 single hands punches with the left hand and right hand (Total 80 punches)

e. check every week the speed of every individual kicks in 1 minute and make a table of improvement (minimum kicks must be 120 kicks in 1 minute in Air every week)

SQUATS KICKS

Sunday Body Weight Squats Kicks below following kicks

2nd & 3rd week schedule

Sit on squat and get up and kick Down heel kick with one squat 2 kicks with the Right leg and left leg and sit. Do 8 kicks each leg (i.e. Total 16 kicks) in 1 minute.

Sit on squat and get up and kick inner edge with Right leg and left leg and sit. Do 8 kicks each leg (i.e. Total 16 kicks) in 1 minute.

Sit on squat and get up and kick outer edge with left leg and Right leg and sit. Do 8 kicks each leg (i.e. Total 16 kicks) in 1 minute.

Sit on squat and get up and kick front thrust kick with Right leg and with the Left leg and sit. Do 8 kicks each leg (i.e. Total 16 kicks) in 1 minute.

Sit on squat and get up and kick side kick with Right leg and with the Left leg and sit. Do 8 kicks each leg (i.e. Total 16 kicks) in 1 minute.

Sit on squat and get up and kick front side kick with Right leg and with the Left leg and sit. Do 8 kicks each leg (i.e. Total 16 kicks) in 1 minute.

Sit on squat and get up and kick Round house kick with Left leg and with the Right leg and sit. Do 8 kicks each leg (i.e. Total 16 kicks) in 1 minute.

Sit on squat and get up and kick Back kick with Right leg and with the Left leg and sit. Do 8 kicks each leg (i.e. Total 16 kicks) in 1 minute.

Sit on squat and get up and kick Hook kick with Left leg and with the Right leg and sit. Do 8 kicks each leg (i.e. Total 16 kicks) in 1 minute.

3rd Week

Speed Training schedule for 15 Years and above

Speed Training schedule for 13 – 15 Years

Speed Training schedule for below 13 years

"All speed practices are useless when it is not perfect in speed"

\- Grand Master M. Jayanth Reddy

SPEED TRAINING OF KICKS- 15 YEAR AND ABOVE

Monday –I 3rd week schedule

1kg ANKLE (LEG) WEIGHTS KICKS(Alternative Legs)

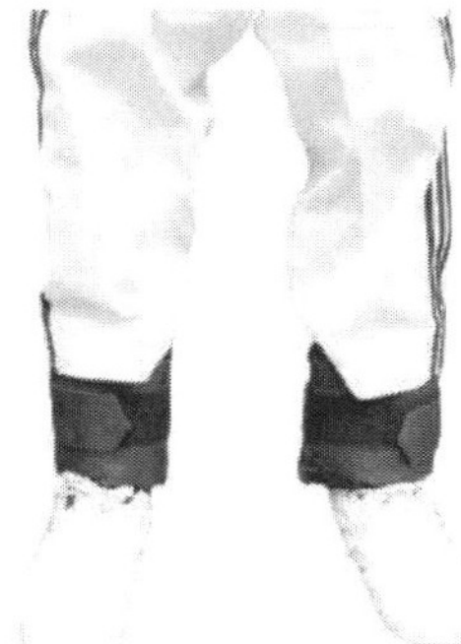

Wear a Ankle weight to your leg 1 kg each leg and start kicking all the kicks as shown in the pictures below. Each kick you need to do a minimum of 20 kicks each leg in 1 minute Rest for 1 minute. Do all 1 to 10 kicks.

1.DOWN HEEL KICK, ALTERNATIVE LEGS

2.SIDE KICK, ALTERNATIVE LEGS

3. SPINNING CART WHEEL KICK, ALTERNATIVE LEGS

4. HOOK KICK, ALTERNATIVE LEGS

5. TRUST KICK ALTENATIVE LEG

6. INNER EDGE KICKS ALTERNATIVE LEGS

7. FRONT SIDE KICKS ALTERNATIVE LEGS

8. ROUND HOUSE KICK ALTERNATIVE LEGS

9. OUTER EDGE KICK ALTERNATIVE LEGS

10. BACK KICK AND DO ALTERNATIVE LEG

II. 1kgs of Ankle Weight kick Controlling:

Do only 4 Kicks i.e., (1) Thrust Kick (2) Side Kick (3) Round House Kick (4) Back Kick Control Each Leg at hips minimum do control for 15 to 20 seconds without any support. See Picture A,B,C and D. Do 2 sets each.

Pic-A

Thrust Kick, Alternative Legs

Pic-B

Side Kick, Alternative

Pic-C

Round House Kick Alternative

Pic-D

Back Kick to with Alternative Leg

III. Sitting kicks with 1 kg Ankle Weight:

Do only 4 kicks (1) snap kicks (2) Side kick (3) Round house kick (4) Hook kick.
Do each kick 70 times alternative legs Lie down on back and wear 1 kgs Ankle weight and kick continuously snap kicks for 30 to 35 kicks see pic-P1 ,pic- P2 and p3.

Pic-P1

Pic-P2

Pic-P3

Kneel led down and sit and hands support on the ground and raise your Right leg Right side and kick side kick continuously 30 to 35 kicks with wearing 1kg Ankle weights and change the leg and do with other leg same. See pic-P4 and pic-P5.

pic-P4

pic-P5

Kneel led down and sit and hands support on the ground and kick round house kick sideways 30 to 35 times each leg with wearing 1kgs Ankle weight. See pic-P6 and pic-P7

pic-P6

pic-P7

Kneel led down and sit and hands support on the ground and kick Hook kick sideways 30 to 35 times each leg wearing 1kgs Ankle weight. See pic-P8 and pic-P9.

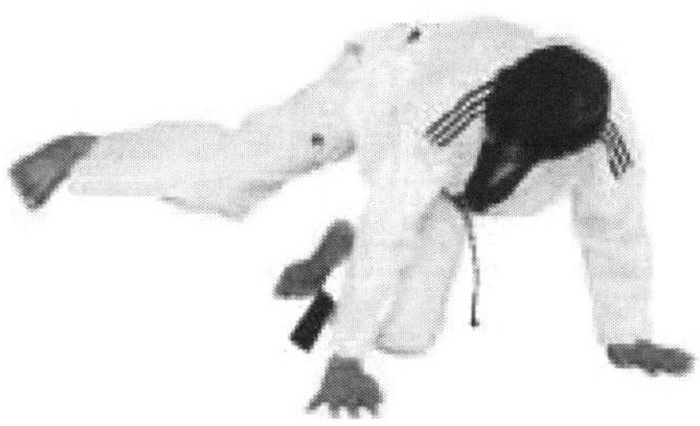

pic-P8

pic-P9

SPEED TRAINING OF PUNCHES - 15 YEAR AND ABOVE

Monday –I 3rd week schedule

1kg HAND WEIGHTS (Alternative Hands)

(a) Horse stand Horse stand and hold 1 kg hand weight and Do 75 punches with alternative hands with 1kg hand weight in 1 minute See picture 1 and 2

Pic -1

Pic -2

(b) Stand in front forward stance and punch with single Right hand over the left open hand (Bend at elbow in the front) 35 punches with Single hand with 1kg hand weight in 1 minute

And change the hand i.e. change to left hand And punch with the same as Right hand punch.

See picture 3,4,5 and 6

Pic -3

Pic -4

Pic -5

Pic -6

(c) Speed sitting hand weights punches Sit on chair or stool and punch at least 60 times with alternative hand (with left hand and right hand)

Variation: your can do this sitting punches by blind folded i.e. with closing eyes, by imagining you are smashing with punch. See picture 7 and 8

Pic -7

Pic -8

(D) Biceps Forearm Triceps Strengthening Exercises for Speed

Bicep Exercise 1

Hold 10 pounds in left hand and pull till chest. This will strengthen the biceps. Do with other hand each 3 sets of 10 times. Refer pictures A, B , A1 and B1

Pic -A

Pic -B

Pic -A1

Pic - B1

Bicep Exercise 2

Sit on chair and take 10 pounds hand dumbbell and pull up to chest level 10 repetitions each hand alternatively. Refer pictures A, B, C and D.

Pic -A

Pic -B

Pic -B

Pic -D

Triceps Strengthening 3

Horse stance with barbell weight back of you and slightly bend forward your upper body and lift weight 10 pounds. See picture A.

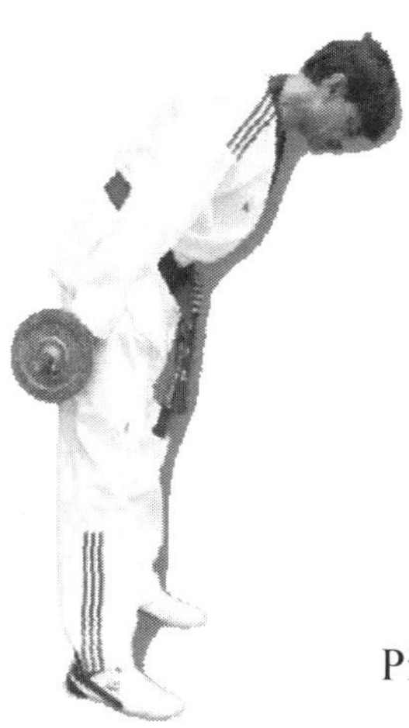

Pic - A

Biceps Strengthening 4

Stand with barbell weight on your hand forward pull weight up to chest and withdraw to thighs. Do with 15 pounds increases according to your capacity. Do at least 10 repetitions Do 2 sets. . See picture A.

Pic -A

Forearm Exercise 5

Forearm and wrist strengthening

Stand with holding one sided dumbbell 5 pounds (approximately) sideways should be besides you and pull up as high as possible, Front side. Do with left hand and with right hand. This exercise will strengthen wrist, forearm. See pictures A, B, A1 and B1.

Pic - A

Pic - B

Pic – A1

Pic – B1

Forearm Strengthening Exercise 6

Stand with holding one sided dumbbell 5 pounds (approximately) with right hand beside your thigh and pull up and down back side 10 times each hand alternately. See picture C and D.

Pic - C

Pic - D

Wrist Strengthening Exercises7

Sit on chair and hold one side dumbbell 5 pounds (approximately) with Right forearm on the thighs and twist to left and right side with maximum strain. Do with other hand, Do 10 times each. See pictures A, B,C,D,E,F

Pic -A

Pic - B

Pic - C

Pic -D

Pic - E

Pic - F

Triceps Exercise 8

Sit on chair and hold one side Drum bell 5 pounds with Right hand Back side and pull up and Down, See pictures S1, S2, S3, and S4

Pic – S1

Pic – S2

Pic – S3

Pic – S4

Forearm Strengthening 9

Sit on stool and holding bar with 5 pounds (approximately) weight with palm facing sky, as shown in picture with hands 10" inches apart and pull up your wrist to you and pull down 10 times. Note: Keep forearm and elbow on the thighs to balance the weight. See pictures A and B.

Pic – A

Pic - B

Forearm strengthening 10

Sit on stool and holding bar 5 pounds (approximately) as shown in picture with hands 10" inches apart and pull to you and pull down 10 times. Note: Keep forearm and elbow on the thighs to balance the weight with palm facing floor in punching position. See pictures C and D.

Pic – C

Pic – D

Forearm Strengthening Exercises 11

Holding 12" to 15" long rod 5 pounds (approximately) tightly on the right side and twist 180degrees for 15 times and change the hand and continue. See pictures A, B, C

Variations: You can hold 2 rods either side of each hand and twist them.

Pic - A

Pic - B

Pic - C

Forearm Strengthening 12

Hold 12" to 14" rod 5 pounds (approximately) in front of you and twist left and right 180 degrees angle with left hand 15 times repetitions and change to right hand and do the same repetitions. See pictures A, B, C, D, E and F.

Pic - A

Pic – B

Pic – C

Pic- D

Pic – E

Pic - F

Triceps Strengthening Exercise 13

Keep index and thumb of each hand join together and go for pushups with leg stretch out without bending knees. Do this exercise for 10 times daily. See pictures A and B.

Pic A

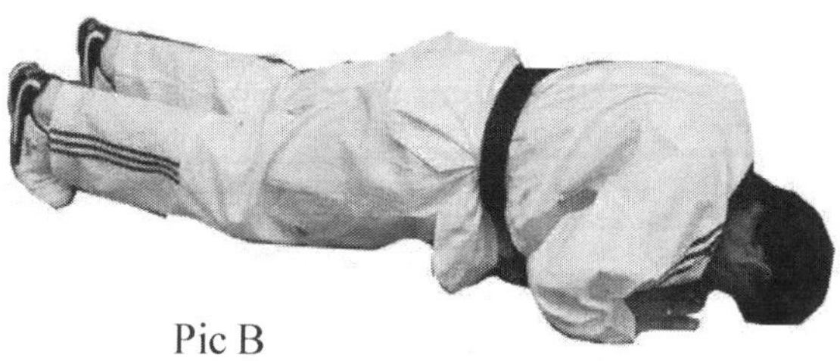

Pic B

Friday: Same as on Monday Schedule

SPEED PEDDLE KICKS(kicking on pad)

Tuesday 3rd week schedule

I. PAD KICKING EACH LEG 25 KICKS 1 TO 15 KICKS

(1) Push kick

(2) Front thrust kick

(3) Side kick

(4) Round house kick

(5) Back kick

(6) Outer edge kick

(7) Inner edge kick

(8) Down heel kick

(9) Hook kick

(10) Jumping side kick

(11) Jumping Round house kick

(12) Jumping Back kick

(13) Spin kick

(14) Jumping spin kick

(15) Scissor kick

Jumping thrust kick

Push Kick on Pad -1

Front thrust kick on pad -2

Side kick on pad -3

Round house on pad-4

Back kick on pad – 5

Outer edge kick on pad – 6

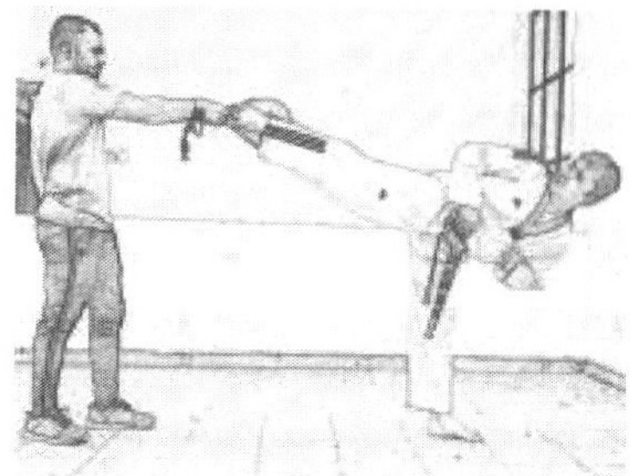

Inner edge kick on pad -7 Down heel kick on pad -8 Hook kick on pad – 9

Jumping side kick on pad – 10 Jumping Round house kick on pad - 11 Jumping Back kick on pad – 12

Jumping spin kick on pad - 13

Front Side kick -14

Scissor kick-15

II. PAD KICKING LEFT LEG 20 KICKS IN 30 SECONDS SINGLE LEG

III. PAD KICKING RIGHT LEG 20 KICKS IN 30 SECONDS SINGLE LEG

Note: I,II and III Rest for 1 minutes of each kick, Do all kicks accordingly

Thursday: Same as on Tuesday Schedule

SPEED NYLON / TUBE KICKING

Wednesday 3rd week schedule

Speed Kicking With Tube

Tie bicycle tube or nylon thread and tie to your ankle and kick all kicks 20 times in 30 seconds alternative leg. Rest for 1 minute with each kick.
Do all kicks below mentioned stationary kicks 20 kicks in 30 seconds and 10 jumping kicks in 20 seconds.

Speed Kicking With Tube

Tie bicycle tube or nylon thread and tie to your ankle and kick all kicks 22 times with each leg. This improves kicking speed. Once in a week you can do single leg kick and alternative leg kicks.

Side Kick with Left

Side Kick with Right

Hook

Outer edge kick

Round house kick

Thrust kick

Back kick

Back kick

Jumping Round house kick

Jumping side kick with Right leg

Jumping side kick with Left leg

SPEED KICKING ON PAD WITH TIEING TUBE

Down heel kick with tube

Inner edge kick with tube

Outer edge kick with tube

Front thrust kick with tube

Round house kick with tube

Side kick with tube

Back kick with tube

Hook kick with tube

Jumping Round house kick with tube

Jumping Back kick with tube

Jumping side kick with tube

Jumping thrust kick with tube

Turning Jumping Round house
kick with tube Pic -A1

Turning Jumping Round house
kick with tube pic-A2

Turning Jumping Round house kick
with tube Pic -A3

WEDNESDAY: **SPEED TRAINING OF PUNCHES**

3rd week schedule

(iii) Knuckle pushups, Close fist and keep knuckle on ground with shoulder width distance and go down and come up. Do 15 push ups and 90 punches in 1 minute. See pictures A and B and C

Pic - A

Pic- C

Pic - B

(ii) Single hand knuckle pushups: Do one hand knuckle pushups 10 times one hand 30 punches in 1 minute and Change knuckles. Do alternate hands Do 2 sets. See picture A

Pic - A

(iii) Power pushups for speed & power punches:

Sit on kneeling position with palms facing ground and jump forward onto your palms on the floor as shown in pictures A and B. Do 5 sets and get up and Do 100 punches in 1 minute.

Pic -A

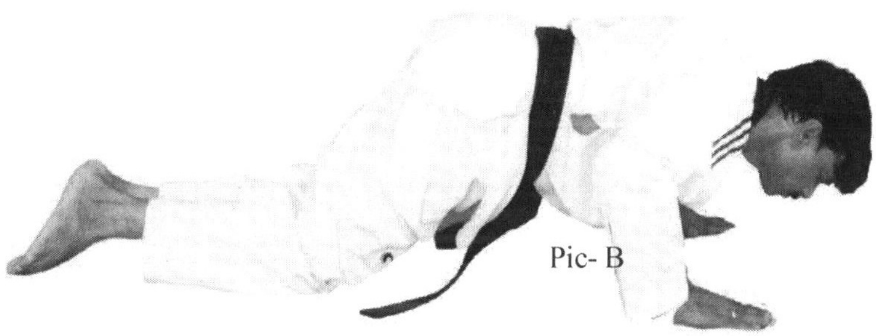

Pic- B

(iv) Pushing the kit bag and speed punch exercise: pushing the kit bag and 2 hands punches alternatively .Do 20 sets See pic- P1, P2 and P3

Pic –P1

Pic –P2

Pic –P3

Saturday: Tube kicking with single leg

3rd week schedule

Tube kicking with single leg 25 kicks in 30 seconds one minute Rest between each single leg kicks

Do all kicks 25 times in 30 seconds each leg. Below mention kicks.

Side Kick with Left

Side Kick with Right

Hook

Outer edge kick

Round house kick

Thrust kick

Back kick

Back kick

Jumping Round house kick

SPEED UNDER WATER KICKS & UNDER WATER PUNCHES

Sunday 3rd week schedule, water workout (water must be chest level)

I. Under water kicks Do 1 to 8 kicks each leg 8 kicks (total 16 kicks) in 1 minute

1.Inner edge kick

2.Thrust kick

3.Side kick

4.Spinning kick

5.Round house kick

6. Hook kick

7. Outer edge kick

8. Hook kick and side kick with holding wall

II. a. Running in the water :
Running in the water 20 meters

b. Side Running in the water :
Running in the water right side 20 meters and left side 20 meters

c. knee raising in the water :
Knee raising in the water each leg 40 times (Total 80 times)

d. punches in the water :
(i)75double punches in the water with alternative hands
(ii)60single hands punches with the left hand and right hand (Total 120 punches)

e. check the speed of every individual kicks in 1 minute and make a of table improvement (minimum kicks must be 100 kicks in 1 minute)

f. check the speed of every individual kicks in 1 minute and make a of table improvement

SQUATS KICKS

Sunday Body Weight Squats Kicks below following kicks

3rd week schedule

Sit on squat and get up and kick Down heel kick with one squat 2 kicks the Right leg and left leg and sit. Do 8 kicks each leg (i.e. Total 16 kicks) See pic-L1,pic-L2,pic-L3 and pic-4

Pic-L1

Pic-L2

Pic-L3

Pic-L4

Sit on squat and get up and kick inner edge with Right leg and left leg and sit. Do 8 kicks each leg (i.e. Total 16 kicks) see pic- L5 and pic-L6.

Sit on squat and get up and kick outer edge with left leg and Right leg and sit. Do 8 kicks each leg (i.e. Total 16 kicks) See pic- L7 and pic-L8.

Sit on squat and get up and kick front thrust kick with Right leg and with the Left leg and sit. Do 8 kicks each leg (i.e. Total 16 kicks) See pic-L9 and pic-L10

Pic-L5

Pic-L6

Pic-L7

Pic-L8

Pic-L9

Pic-L10

Sit on squat and get up and kick side kick with Right leg and with the Left leg and sit. Do 8 kicks each leg (i.e. Total 16 kicks) See pic-L11 and pic-L12.

Sit on squat and get up and kick front side kick with Right leg and with the Left leg and sit. Do 8 kicks each leg (i.e. Total 16 kicks) See pic-L13 and pic-L14.

Sit on squat and get up and kick Round house kick with Left leg and with the Right leg and sit. Do 8 kicks each leg (i.e. Total 16 kicks) See pic-L15 and pic-L16.

Pic-L11

Pic-L12

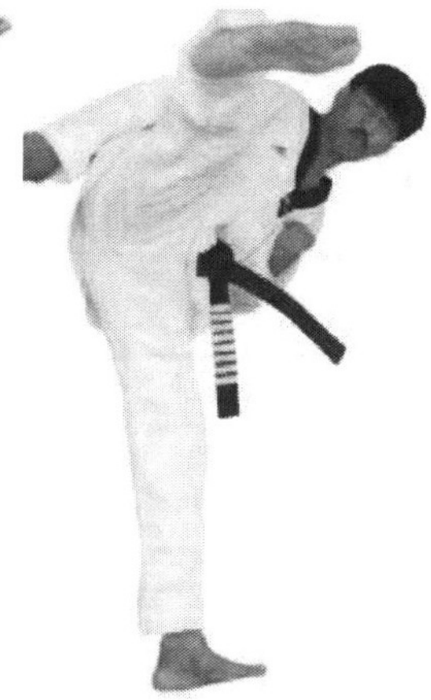

Pic-L13

Pic-L14

Pic-L15

Pic-L16 (side view)

Sit on squat and get up and kick Back kick with Right leg and with the Left leg and sit. Do 8 kicks each leg (i.e. Total 16 kicks) See pic-L17,pic-L18 and L19 Back kick in Front View.

Pic-L17

Pic-L18

Back kick Front view Pic-L19

Sit on squat and get up and kick Hook kick with Left leg and with the Right leg and sit. Do 8 kicks each leg (i.e. Total 16 kicks) See pic-L20,pic-L21 Front view.

Pic-L20 (Side View)

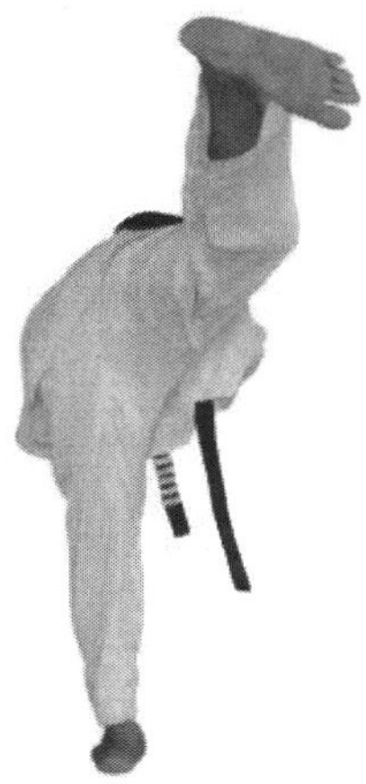

Hook kick front viewPic-L21

SPEED TRAINING OF KICKS-13 TO 15 YEARS

Monday –I 3rd week schedule

½ kg ANKLE (LEG) WEIGHTS KICKS (Alternative Legs)

Wear a Ankle weight to your leg 1/2 kg each leg and start kicking all the kicks as shown in the pictures below. Each kick you need to do a minimum of 40 kicks each leg in 1 minute Rest for 2 minute. Do all 1 to 10 kicks.

1. down heel kick, alternative legs
2. Side Kick, alternative Legs
3. Spinning cart wheel kick, alternative legs
4. Hook Kick, alternative Legs
5. Trust Kick alternative Leg
6. Inner edge kicks alternative legs
7. Front side kicks alternative legs
8. Round House Kick Alternative Legs
9. Outer Edge Kick Alternative Legs
10. Back Kick and Do Alternative Leg

II. ½ kgs of Ankle Weight kick Controlling:

Do only 4 Kicks i.e., (1) Thrust Kick (2) Side Kick (3) Round House Kick (4) Back Kick

Control Each Leg at hips minimum do control for 25 seconds without any support.

III. Sitting kicks with ½ kg Ankle Weight:

Do only 4 kicks (1) snap kicks (2) Side kick (3) Round house kick (4) Hook kick.
Do each kick 70 times alternative legs Lie down on back and wear 1kgs Ankle weight and kick continuously snap kicks for 70 kicks

Kneel Led down and sit and hands support on the ground and raise your Right leg Right side and kick side kick continuously 30 kicks with wearing 1kg Ankle weights and change the leg and do with other leg same.

Kneel Led down and sit and hands support on the ground and kick round house kick sideways 30 times each leg with wearing 1kgs Ankle weight.

Kneel Led down and sit and hands support on the ground and kick Hook kick sideways 30 times each leg wearing 1kg Ankle weight

SPEED TRAINING OF PUNCHES - 13 TO 15 YEARS

Monday –I 3rd week schedule

300 grams HAND WEIGHTS (Alternative Hands)

(a) Horse stand and hold 300grams hand weight and Do 60 punches with alternative hands in 1 minute

(b) Stand in front forward stance and punch with single Right hand over the left open hand (Bend at elbow in the front) 20 punches with Single hand with 300 grams hand weight in 1 minute
And change the hand i.e. change to left hand and punch with the same as Right hand punch.

(c) Speed sitting hand weights punches Sit on chair or stool and punch at least 40 times with alternative hand (with left hand and right hand)
Variation: your can do this sitting punches by blind folded i.e. with closing eyes, by imagining you are smashing with punch.

(d) Forearm Exercise
Forearm and wrist strengthening
Stand with holding one sided dumbbell 5 pounds (approximately) sideways should be besides you and pull up as high as possible, Front side. Do with left hand and with right hand. This exercise will strengthen wrist, forearm.

(e) Forearm Strengthening Exercise
Stand with holding one sided dumbbell 5 pounds (approximately) with right hand beside your thigh and pull up and down back side 12 times each hand alternately.

(f) Wrist Strengthening Exercises
Sit on chair and hold one side dumbbell 5 pounds (approximately) with Right forearm on the thighs and twist to left and right side with maximum strain. Do with other hand, Do 10 times each.

(g) Forearm Strengthening
Sit on stool and holding bar with 10 pounds (approximately) weight with palm facing sky, as shown in picture with hands 10" inches apart and pull up your wrist to you and pull down 12 times. Note: Keep forearm and elbow on the thighs to balance the weight

(h) Forearm strengthening
Sit on stool and holding bar10 pounds (approximately) as shown in picture with hands 10" inches apart and pull to you and pull down 10 times. Note: Keep forearm and elbow on the thighs to balance the weight with palm facing floor in punching position

(i)Forearm Strengthening Exercises
Holding 12" to 15" long rod 5 pounds (approximately) tightly on the right side and twist 180 degrees for 20 times and change the hand and continue.
Variations: You can hold 2 rods either side of each hand and twist them.

(j)Forearm Strengthening
Hold 12" to 14" rod 5 pounds (approximately) in front of you and twist left and right 180 degrees angle with left hand 18 repetitions and change to right hand and do the same repetitions.

(k) Triceps Strengthening Exercise
Keep index and thumb of each hand join together and go for pushups with leg stretch out without bending knees. Do this exercise for 10 times daily.

Friday: Same as on Monday Schedule

SPEED PEDDLE KICKS(kicking on pad)
Tuesday 3rd week schedule

I. PAD KICKING EACH LEG 20 KICKS 1 TO 15 KICKS

(1) Push kick

(2) Front thrust kick

(3) Side kick

(4) Round house kick

(5) Back kick

(6) Outer edge kick

(7) Inner edge kick

(8) Down heel kick

(9) Hook kick

(10) Jumping side kick

(11) Jumping Round house kick

(12) Jumping Back kick

(13) Spin kick

(14) Jumping spin kick

(15) Scissor kick

II. PAD KICKING LEFT LEG 20 KICKS IN 30 SECONDS SINGLE LEG

III. PAD KICKING RIGHT LEG 20 KICKS IN 30 SECONDS SINGLE LEG

Note: I,II and III Rest for 1 ½ minutes of each kick, Do all kicks accordingly

Thursday: Same as on Tuesday Schedule

SPEED NYLON / TUBE KICKING

Wednesday 3rd week schedule

Speed Kicking With Tube

Tie bicycle tube or nylon thread and tie to your ankle and kick all kicks 20 times in 45 seconds alternative leg. Rest for 1 minute with each kick in air or kicking pad.
Do all kicks below mentioned stationary kicks 22 kicks in 45 seconds and 10 jumping kicks in 50 seconds.

Speed Kicking With Tube

Tie bicycle tube or nylon thread and tie to your ankle and kick all kicks 22 times with each leg.
This improves kicking speed. Once in a week you can do single leg kick and alternative leg kicks.
Do below mentioned kicks.

1. Side Kick with Left and Right Leg
2. Outer edge kick with Left and Right Leg
3. Inner edge kick with Left and Right Leg
4. Thrust kick with Left and Right Leg
5. Back kick with Left and Right Leg
6. Round house kick with Left and Right Leg
7. Hook Kick with Left and Right Leg
8. Jumping Round house kick with Left and Right Leg
9. Jumping side kick with Left and Right Leg
10. Down heel kick with Left and Right Leg
11. Jumping Thrust kick with Left and Right Leg
12. Jumping Back kick with Left and Right Leg

WEDNESDAY: <u>SPEED TRAINING OF PUNCHES</u>

3rd week schedule

(i) Knuckle pushups, Close fist and keep knuckle on ground with shoulder width distance and go down and come up. Do 15 push ups and 60 punches in 1 minute.

(ii) Single hand knuckle pushups: Do one hand knuckle pushups 10 times one hand 20 punches in 1 minute and Change knuckles. Do alternate hands Do 2 sets

(iii) Power pushups for speed & power punches
Sit on kneeling position with palms facing ground and jump forward onto your palms on the Floor and Do 3 sets and get up and Do 125 punches in 2 minutes.

(iv) Pushing the kit bag and speed punch exercise: pushing the kit bag and 2 hands punches alternatively .Do 20 sets

Saturday: Tube kicking with single leg

3rd week schedule

Tube kicking with single leg 20 kicks in 45 seconds one minute or 2 minutes Rest between each single leg kicks

Do all kicks 20 times in 45 seconds each leg. Below mentioned kicks.

1. Side Kick with Left and Right Leg
2. Hook Kick with Left and Right Leg
3. Outer edge kick with Left and Right Leg
4. Round house kick with Left and Right Leg
5. *Thrust kick* with Left and Right Leg
6. Back kick with Left and Right Leg
7. Jumping Round house kick with Left and Right Leg
8. Inner edge kick with Left and Right Leg

SPEED UNDER WATER KICKS & UNDER WATER PUNCHES

Sunday 3rd week schedule, water workout (water must be chest level)

I. Under water kicks Do 1 to 8 kicks each leg 10 kicks (total 20 kicks)
Do below mentioned kicks

1.Inner edge kick

2.Thrust kick

3.Side kick

4.Spinning kick

5.Round house kick

6. Hook kick

7. Outer edge kick

8. Hook kick and side kick with holding wall

II. a. Running in the water :
Running in the water 15 meters

b. Side Running in the water :
Running in the water right side 15 meters and left side 15 meters

c. knee raising in the water :
Knee raising in the water each leg 30 times (Total 60 times)

d. punches in the water :
(i)90 double punches in the water with alternative hands
(ii)60 single hands punches with the left hand and right hand (Total 120 punches)

e. check the speed of every individual kicks in 1 minute and make a table of improvement (minimum kicks must be 140 kicks in 1 minute in Air every week)

SQUATS KICKS
Sunday Body Weight Squats Kicks below following kicks
3rd week schedule

Sit on squat and get up and kick Down heel kick with one squat 2 kicks with the Right leg and left leg and sit. Do 8 kicks each leg (i.e. Total 16 kicks)

Sit on squat and get up and kick inner edge with Right leg and left leg and sit. Do 8 kicks each leg (i.e. Total 16kicks).

Sit on squat and get up and kick outer edge with left leg and Right leg and sit. Do 8 kicks each leg (i.e. Total 16 kicks).

Sit on squat and get up and kick front thrust kick with Right leg and with the Left leg and sit. Do 8 kicks each leg (i.e. Total 16 kicks) .

Sit on squat and get up and kick side kick with Right leg and with the Left leg and sit.

Do 8 kicks each leg (i.e. Total 16 kicks).

Sit on squat and get up and kick front side kick with Right leg and with the Left leg and sit. Do 8 kicks each leg (i.e. Total 16 kicks).

Sit on squat and get up and kick Round house kick with Left leg and with the Right leg and sit. Do 8 kicks each leg (i.e. Total 16 kicks).

Sit on squat and get up and kick Back kick with Right leg and with the Left leg and sit. Do 8 kicks each leg (i.e. Total 16 kicks).

Sit on squat and get up and kick Hook kick with Left leg and with the Right leg and sit. Do 8 kicks each leg (i.e. Total 16 kicks).

SPEED TRAINING OF KICKS - BELOW 13 YEARS

Monday –I 2nd & 3rd week schedule

70 KICKS IN 2 MINITUES

Each kick you need to do a minimum of 35 kicks each leg in 1 minute Rest for 2 minute. Do all 1 to 10 kicks. Below mention kicks

1. down heel kick, alternative legs
2. Side Kick, alternative Legs
3. Spinning cart wheel kick, alternative legs
4. Hook Kick, alternative Legs
5. Trust Kick alternative Leg
6. Inner edge kicks alternative legs
7. Front side kicks alternative legs
8. Round House Kick Alternative Legs
9. Outer Edge Kick Alternative Legs
10. Back Kick and Do Alternative Leg

II. Kick Controlling:

Do only 4 Kicks i.e., (1) Thrust Kick (2) Side Kick (3) Round House Kick (4) Back Kick

Control Each Leg at hips minimum do control for 20 to 25 seconds without any support.

III. Sitting kicks:

Do only 4 kicks (1) snap kicks (2) Side kick (3) Round house kick (4) Hook kick.
Do each kick 50 times alternative legs Lie down on back and kick continuously snap kicks start from 25 kicks to 50 kicks

Kneel Led down and sit and hands support on the ground and raise your Right leg Right side and kick side kick continuously 25 to 50 and change the leg and do with other leg same.

Kneel down and sit and hands support on the ground and kick round house kick sideways 25 to 50 times each leg.

Kneel down and sit and hands support on the ground and kick Hook kick sideways 25 to 50 times each leg.

Variation: kicks on x-ray film. You can do all kicks and all punches on x-ray film each kick 10 times and 40 punch with 2 hands.

SPEED TRAINING OF PUNCHES - BELOW 13 YEARS

Monday –I 2nd & 3rd week schedule

120 punches in 1 minute (Alternative Hands)

(a) Horse stand and Do 120 punches with alternative hands in 1 minute Do 2 sets.

(b) Stand in front forward stance and punch with single Right hand over the left open hand (Bend at elbow in the front) 60 punches with Single hand with in 1 minute Do 2 sets And change the hand i.e. change to left hand and punch with the same as Right hand punch.

(c) Speed sitting hand punches Sit on chair or stool and punch at least 80 times with alternative hand (with left hand and right hand) Do 2 sets.
Variation: your can do this sitting punches by blind folded i.e. with closing eyes, by imagining you are smashing with punch.

(d) Punches on x-ray film: you can practices 60 with each hand (total 120 punches)

(e) Triceps Strengthening Exercise
Keep index and thumb of each hand join together and go for pushups with leg stretch out without bending knees. Do this exercise for 8 to 10 times daily.

Friday: Same as on Monday Schedule

SPEED PEDDLE KICKS(kicking on pad)

Tuesday 2nd &3rd week schedule

I. PAD KICKING EACH LEG 20 KICKS 1 TO 15 KICKS

(1) Push kick - 20 kicks each leg
(2) Front thrust kick " "
(3) Side kick " "
(4) Round house kick " "
(5) Back kick " "
(6) Outer edge kick " "
(7) Inner edge kick " "
(8) Down heel kick " "
(9) Hook kick " "
(10) Jumping side kick " "
(11) Jumping Round house kick " "

(12) Jumping Back kick - 12 kicks each leg

(13) Spin kick -20 kicks each leg

(14) Jumping spin kick -12 kicks each leg

(15) Scissor kick - 20 kicks each leg

II. PAD KICKING LEFT LEG 20 KICKS IN 1MINITE SINGLE LEG

III. PAD KICKING RIGHT LEG 20 KICKS IN 1MINITE SINGLE LEG

Note: I,II and III Rest for 1 ½ minutes of each kick, Do all kicks accordingly

Thursday: Same as on Tuesday Schedule

WEDNESDAY: SPEED TRAINING OF PUNCHES

2nd & 3rd week schedule

(i) Knuckle pushups, Close fist and keep knuckle on ground with shoulder width distance and go down and come up or palms pushups Do 10 pushups and 50 punches in 1 minute.

(ii) Single hand knuckle or palms pushups: Do one hand knuckle pushups 10 times one hand 30 punches in 1 minute and Change knuckles. Do alternate hands Do 2 sets

(iii) Power pushups for speed & power punches
Sit on kneeling position with palms facing ground and jump forward onto your palms on the Floor and Do 3 sets and get up and Do 125 punches in 2 minutes.

(iv) Pushing the kit bag and speed punch exercise: pushing the kit bag and 2 hands punches alternatively .Do 20 sets

SPEED UNDER WATER KICKS & UNDER WATER PUNCHES

Sunday 2nd & 3rd week schedule, water workout (water must be chest level)

II. Under water kicks Do 1 to 8 kicks each leg 8 kicks (total 16 kicks) in 1 minute
Do below mentioned kicks

1.Inner edge kick

2.Thrust kick

3.Side kick

4.Spinning kick

5.Round house kick

6. Hook kick

7. Outer edge kick

8. Hook kick and side kick with holding wall

II. a. Running in the water :
Running in the water 10 meters

b. Side Running in the water :
Running in the water right side 10 meters and left side 10 meters

c. knee raising in the water :
Knee raising in the water each leg 25 times (Total 50 times)

d. punches in the water :
(i) 50 double punches in the water with alternative hands
(ii)40 single hands punches with the left hand and right hand (Total 80 punches)

e. check every week the speed of every individual kicks in 1 minute and make a table of improvement (minimum kicks must be 120 kicks in 1 minute in Air every week)

SQUATS KICKS

Sunday Body Weight Squats Kicks below following kicks
2nd & 3rd week schedule

Sit on squat and get up and kick Down heel kick with one squat 2 kicks with the Right leg and left leg and sit. Do 8 kicks each leg (i.e. Total 16 kicks) in 1 minute.

Sit on squat and get up and kick inner edge with Right leg and left leg and sit. Do 8 kicks each leg (i.e. Total 16 kicks) in 1 minute.

Sit on squat and get up and kick outer edge with left leg and Right leg and sit. Do 8 kicks each leg (i.e. Total 16 kicks) in 1 minute.

Sit on squat and get up and kick front thrust kick with Right leg and with the Left leg and sit. Do 8 kicks each leg (i.e. Total 16 kicks) in 1 minute.

Sit on squat and get up and kick side kick with Right leg and with the Left leg and sit. Do 8 kicks each leg (i.e. Total 16 kicks) in 1 minute.

Sit on squat and get up and kick front side kick with Right leg and with the Left leg and sit. Do 8 kicks each leg (i.e. Total 16 kicks) in 1 minute.

Sit on squat and get up and kick Round house kick with Left leg and with the Right leg and sit. Do 8 kicks each leg (i.e. Total 16 kicks) in 1 minute.

Sit on squat and get up and kick Back kick with Right leg and with the Left leg and sit. Do 8 kicks each leg (i.e. Total 16 kicks) in 1 minute.

Sit on squat and get up and kick Hook kick with Left leg and with the Right leg and sit. Do 8 kicks each leg (i.e. Total 16 kicks) in 1 minute.

4 Th Week

Speed Training schedule for 15 Years and above

Speed Training schedule for 13 – 15 Years

Speed Training schedule for below 13 years

"Burning my body when I practice, till the fuel of competition lighted"

- Grand Master M. Jayanth Reddy

SPEED TRAINING OF KICKS- 15 YEAR AND ABOVE

Monday –I 4th week schedule

1kg ANKLE (LEG) WEIGHTS KICKS(Alternative Legs)

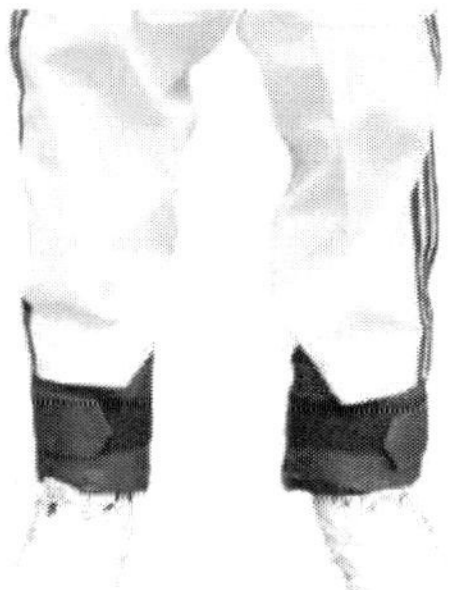

Wear a Ankle weight to your leg 1 kg each leg and start kicking all the kicks as shown in the pictures below. Each kick you need to do a minimum of 25 kicks each leg in 1 minute Rest for 2 minute. Do all 1 to 10 kicks.

1.DOWN HEEL KICK, ALTERNATIVE LEGS

2.SIDE KICK, ALTERNATIVE LEGS

3.SPINNING CART WHEEL KICK, ALTERNATIVE LEGS

4.HOOK KICK, ALTERNATIVE LEGS

5.TRUST KICK ALTENATIVE LEG

6. INNER EDGE KICKS ALTERNATIVE LEGS

7. FRONT SIDE KICKS ALTERNATIVE LEGS

8. ROUND HOUSE KICK ALTERNATIVE LEGS

9. OUTER EDGE KICK ALTERNATIVE LEGS

10. BACK KICK AND DO ALTERNATIVE LEG

II. 1kg of Ankle Weight kick Controlling:

Do only 4 Kicks i.e., (1) Thrust Kick (2) Side Kick (3) Round House Kick (4) Back Kick Control Each Leg at hips minimum do control for 15 to 20 seconds without any support. See Picture A,B,C and D. Do 2 sets each.

Pic-A

Thrust Kick, Alternative Legs

Pic-B

Side Kick, Alternative

Pic-C

Round House Kick Alternative

Pic-D

Back Kick do with Alternative Leg

III. Sitting kicks with 1 kg Ankle Weight:

Do only 4 kicks (1) snap kicks (2) Side kick (3) Round house kick (4) Hook kick.
Do each kick 80 times alternative legs Lie down on back and wear 1 kg Ankle weight and kick continuously snap kicks for 35 to 40 kicks see pic-P1 ,pic- P2 and p3.

Pic-P1

Pic-P2

Pic-P3

Kneel led down and sit and hands support on the ground and raise your Right leg Right side and kick side kick continuously 35 to 40 kicks with wearing 1kg Ankle weights and change the leg and do with other leg same. See pic-P4 and pic-P5.

pic-P4

pic-P5

Kneel led down and sit and hands support on the ground and kick round house kick sideways 35 to 40 times each leg with wearing 1kg Ankle weight. See pic-P6 and pic-P7

pic-P6

pic-P7

Kneel led down and sit and hands support on the ground and kick Hook kick sideways 35 to 40 times each leg wearing 1kg Ankle weight. See pic-P8 and pic-P9.

pic-P8

pic-P9

SPEED TRAINING OF PUNCHES - 15 YEAR AND ABOVE

Monday –I 4th week schedule

1kg HAND WEIGHTS (Alternative Hands)

(a) Horse stand Horse stand and hold 1 kg hand weight and Do 90 punches with alternative hands with 1kg hand weight in 1 minute See picture 1 and 2

(b) Stand in front forward stance and punch with single Right hand over the left open hand(Bend at elbow in the front) 40 punches with Single hand with 1kg hand weight in 1 minute

And change the hand i.e. change to left hand And punch with the same as Right hand punch.

See picture 3,4,5 and 6

Pic -3

Pic -4

Pic -5

Pic -6

(c) Speed sitting hand weights punches Sit on chair or stool and punch at least 70 times with alternative hand (with left hand and right hand)

Variation: your can do this sitting punches by blind folded i.e. with closing eyes, by imagining you are smashing with punch. See picture 7 and 8

Pic -7

Pic -8

(D) Biceps Forearm Triceps Strengthening Exercises for Speed

Bicep Exercise 1

Hold 10 pounds in left hand and pull till chest. This will strengthen the biceps. Do with other hand each 3 sets of 20 times. Refer pictures A, B , A1 and B1

Pic -A Pic -B Pic -A1 Pic - B1

Bicep Exercise 2

Sit on chair and take 15 pounds hand dumbbell and pull up to chest level 20 repetitions each hand alternatively. Refer pictures A, B, C and D.

Pic -A Pic -B Pic -B Pic -D

Triceps Strengthening 3

Horse stance with barbell weight back of you and slightly bend forward your upper body and lift weight 15 pounds. See picture A.

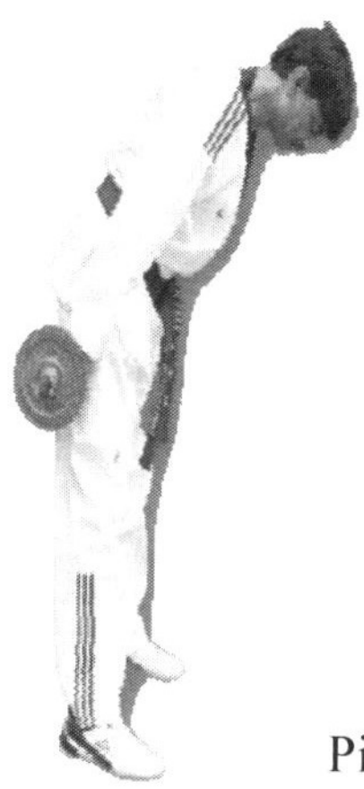

Pic - A

Biceps Strengthening 4

Stand with barbell weight on your hand forward pull weight up to chest and withdraw to thighs. Do with 20 pounds increases according to your capacity. Do at least 20 repetitions Do 3 sets. . See picture A.

Pic -A

Forearm Exercise 5

Forearm and wrist strengthening

Stand with holding one sided dumbbell 8 pounds (approximately) sideways should be besides you and pull up as high as possible, Front side. Do with left hand and with right hand. This exercise will strengthen wrist, forearm. See pictures A, B, A1 and B1.

Pic - A Pic - B Pic – A1 Pic – B1

Forearm Strengthening Exercise 6

Stand with holding one sided dumbbell 8 pounds (approximately) with right hand beside your thigh and pull up and down back side 20 times each hand alternately. See picture C and D.

Pic - C

Pic - D

Wrist Strengthening Exercises7

Sit on chair and hold one side dumbbell 8 pounds (approximately) with Right forearm on the thighs and twist to left and right side with maximum strain. Do with other hand, Do 15 times each. See pictures A, B,C,D,E,F

Pic -A

Pic - B

Pic - C

Pic -D

Pic - E

Pic - F

Triceps Exercise 8

Sit on chair and hold one side Drum bell 8 to 10 pounds (approximately) with Right hand Back side and pull up and Down, See pictures S1, S2, S3, and S4

Pic – S1

Pic – S2

Pic – S3

Pic – S4

Forearm Strengthening 9

Sit on stool and holding bar with 15 pounds (approximately) weight with palm facing sky, as shown in picture with hands 10" inches apart and pull up your wrist to you and pull down 20 times. Note: Keep forearm and elbow on the thighs to balance the weight. See pictures A and B.

Pic – A

Pic-B

Pic – A

Forearm strengthening 10

Sit on stool and holding bar15 pounds (approximately) as shown in picture with hands 10" inches apart and pull to you and pull down 20 times. Note: Keep forearm and elbow on the thighs to balance the weight with palm facing floor in punching position. See pictures C and D.

Pic – C

Pic – D

Forearm Strengthening Exercises 11

Holding 12" to 15" long rod 8 pounds (approximately) tightly on the right side and twist 180degrees for 30 times and change the hand and continue. See pictures A, B, C

Variations: You can hold 2 rods either side of each hand and twist them.

Pic - A

Pic - B

Pic - C

Forearm Strengthening 12

Hold 12" to 14" rod 8 pounds (approximately) in front of you and twist left and right 180 degrees angle with left hand 20 to 30 repetitions and change to right hand and do the same repetitions. See pictures A, B, C, D, E and F.

Pic - A Pic – B Pic – C Pic- D Pic – E Pic - F

Triceps Strengthening Exercise 13

Keep index and thumb of each hand join together and go for pushups with leg stretch out without bending knees. Do this exercise for 10 to 20 times daily. See pictures A and B.

Pic A

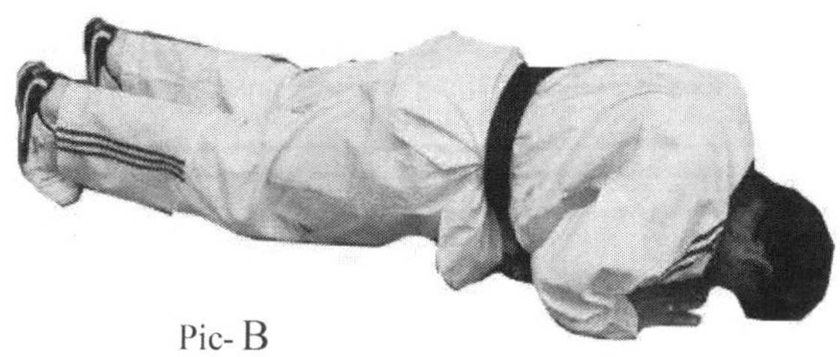

Pic- B

Friday: Same as on Monday Schedule

SPEED PEDDLE KICKS(kicking on pad)

Tuesday 4th week schedule

I. PAD KICKING EACH LEG 30 KICKS 1 TO 15 KICKS

(1) Push kick

(2) Front thrust kick

(3) Side kick

(4) Round house kick

(5) Back kick

(6) Outer edge kick

(7) Inner edge kick

(8) Down heel kick

(9) Hook kick

(10) Jumping side kick

(11) Jumping Round house kick

(12) Jumping Back kick

(13) Spin kick

(14) Jumping spin kick

(15) Scissor kick

Jumping thrust kick

Push Kick on Pad -1

Front thrust kick on pad -2

Side kick on pad -3

Round house on pad-4

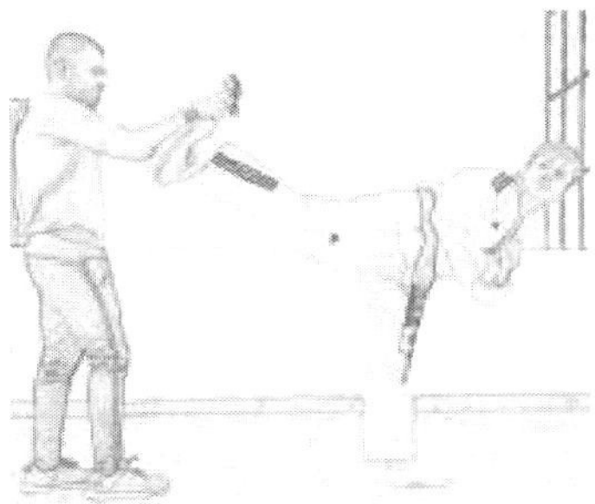

Back kick on pad – 5

Outer edge kick on pad – 6

Inner edge kick on pad -7

Down heel kick on pad -8

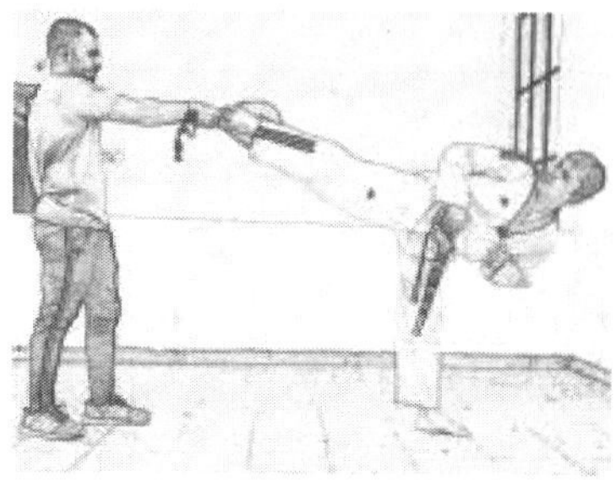

Hook kick on pad – 9

Jumping side kick on pad – 10

Jumping Round house kick on pad - 11

Jumping Back kick on pad – 12

Jumping spin kick on pad - 13

Front Side kick -14

Scissor kick-15

II. PAD KICKING LEFT LEG 30 KICKS IN 30 SECONDS SINGLE LEG

III. PAD KICKING RIGHT LEG 30 KICKS IN 30 SECONDS SINGLE LEG

Note: I,II and III Rest for 1 ½ minutes of each kick, Do all kicks accordingly

Thursday: Same as on Tuesday Schedule

SPEED NYLON / TUBE KICKING

Wednesday 4th week schedule

Speed Kicking With Tube

Tie bicycle tube or nylon thread and tie to your ankle and kick all kicks 25 times in 30 seconds alternative leg. Rest for 1 minute with each kick.
Do all kicks below mentioned stationary kicks 25 kicks in 30 seconds and 10 jumping kicks in 30 seconds.

Speed Kicking With Tube

Tie bicycle tube or nylon thread and tie to your ankle and kick all kicks 25 times with each leg.

This improves kicking speed. Once in a week you can do single leg kick and alternative leg kicks.

Side Kick with Left

Side Kick with Right

Hook

Outer edge kick

Round house kick

Thrust kick

Back kick

Back kick

Jumping Round house kick

Jumping side kick with Right leg

Jumping side kick with Left leg

SPEED KICKING ON PAD WITH TIEING TUBE

Down heel kick with tube

Inner edge kick with tube

Outer edge kick with tube

Front thrust kick with tube

Round house kick with tube

Side kick with tube

Back kick with tube

Hook kick with tube

Jumping Round house kick with tube

Jumping Back kick with tube

Jumping side kick with tube

Jumping thrust kick with tube

Turning Jumping Round house
kick with tube Pic -A1

Turning Jumping Round house
kick with tube pic-A2

Turning Jumping Round house kick
with tube Pic -A3

WEDNESDAY: <u>SPEED TRAINING OF PUNCHES</u>

4th week schedule

(iv) Knuckle pushups, Close fist and keep knuckle on ground with shoulder width distance and go down and come up. Do 20 push ups and 100 punches in 1 minute. See pictures A and B and C

Pic - A

Pic- C

Pic - B

(ii) Single hand knuckle pushups: Do one hand knuckle pushups 12 times one hand 35 punches in 1minute and Change knuckles. Do alternate hands Do 2 sets. See picture A

Pic - A

(iii) Power pushups for speed & power punches

Sit on kneeling position with palms facing ground and jump forward onto your palms on the floor as shown in pictures A and B. Do 5 sets and get up and Do 125 punches in 2 minutes.

Pic - A

Pic- B

(iv) Pushing the kit bag and speed punch exercise: pushing the kit bag and 2 hands punches alternatively .Do 30 sets See pic- P1, P2 and P3

Pic –P1

Pic –P2

Pic –P3

Saturday: Tube kicking with single leg

4th week schedule

Tube kicking with single leg 30 kicks in 35 seconds one minute Rest between each single leg kicks

Do all kicks 30 times in 35 seconds each leg. Below mention kicks.

Side Kick with Left

Side Kick with Right

Hook

Outer edge kick

Round house kick

Thrust kick

Back kick

Back kick

Jumping Round house kick

SPEED UNDER WATER KICKS & UNDER WATER PUNCHES

Sunday 4th week schedule, water workout (water must be chest level)

I. Under water kicks Do 1 to 8 kicks each leg 10 kicks (total 20 kicks) in 1 minute

1.Inner edge kick

2.Thrust kick

3.Side kick

4.Spinning kick

5.Round house kick

6. Hook kick

7. Outer edge kick

8. Hook kick and side kick with holding wall

II. a. Running in the water :
Running in the water 20 meters

b. Side Running in the water :
Running in the water right side 20 meters and left side 20 meters

c. knee raising in the water :
Knee raising in the water each leg 40 times (Total 80 times)

d. punches in the water :
(i)100 double punches in the water with alternative hands
(ii)70single hands punches with the left hand and right hand (Total 140 punches)

e. check the speed of every individual kicks in 1 minute and make a of table improvement (minimum kicks must be 120 kicks in 1 minute)

f. check the speed of every individual kicks in 1 minute and make a of table improvement

SQUATS KICKS

Sunday Body Weight Squats Kicks below following kicks

4th week schedule

Sit on squat and get up and kick Down heel kick with one squat 2 kicks the Right leg and left leg and sit. Do 10 kicks each leg (i.e. Total 20 kicks) See pic-L1,pic-L2,pic-L3 and pic-4

Pic-L1

Pic-L2

Pic-L3

Pic-L4

Sit on squat and get up and kick inner edge with Right leg and left leg and sit. Do 10kicks each leg (i.e. Total 20 kicks) see pic- L5 and pic-L6.

Sit on squat and get up and kick outer edge with left leg and Right leg and sit. Do 10 kicks each leg (i.e. Total 20 kicks) See pic- L7 and pic-L8.

Sit on squat and get up and kick front thrust kick with Right leg and with the Left leg and sit. Do 10 kicks each leg (i.e. Total 20 kicks) See pic-L9 and pic-L10

Pic-L5

Pic-L6

Pic-L7

Pic-L8

Pic-L9

Pic-L10

Sit on squat and get up and kick side kick with Right leg and with the Left leg and sit. Do 10 kicks each leg (i.e. Total 20 kicks) See pic-L11 and pic-L12.

Sit on squat and get up and kick front side kick with Right leg and with the Left leg and sit. Do 10 kicks each leg (i.e. Total 20 kicks) See pic-L13 and pic-L14.

Sit on squat and get up and kick Round house kick with Left leg and with the Right leg and sit. Do 10 kicks each leg (i.e. Total 20 kicks) See pic-L15 and pic-L16.

Pic-L11

Pic-L12

Pic-L13

Pic-L14

Pic-L15

Pic-L16 (side view)

Sit on squat and get up and kick Back kick with Right leg and with the Left leg and sit. Do 10 kicks each leg (i.e. Total 20 kicks) See pic-L17,pic-L18 and L19 Back kick in Front View.

Pic-L17

Pic-L18

Back kick Front view Pic-L19

Sit on squat and get up and kick Hook kick with Left leg and with the Right leg and sit. Do 10 kicks each leg (i.e. Total 20 kicks) See pic-L20,pic-L21 Front view.

Pic-L20 (Side View)

Hook kick front viewPic-L21

SPEED TRAINING OF KICKS-13 TO 15 YEARS

Monday –I 4th week schedule

1kg ANKLE (LEG) WEIGHTS KICKS(Alternative Legs)

Wear a Ankle weight to your leg 1 kg each leg and start kicking all the kicks as shown in the pictures below. Each kick you need to do a minimum of 40 kicks each leg in 1 minute Rest for 2 minute. Do all 1 to 10 kicks.

1. down heel kick, alternative legs
2. Side Kick, alternative Legs
3. Spinning cart wheel kick, alternative legs
4. Hook Kick, alternative Legs
5. Trust Kick alternative Leg
6. Inner edge kicks alternative legs
7. Front side kicks alternative legs
8. Round House Kick Alternative Legs
9. Outer Edge Kick Alternative Legs
10. Back Kick and Do Alternative Leg

II. 1kgs of Ankle Weight kick Controlling:

Do only 4 Kicks i.e., (1) Thrust Kick (2) Side Kick (3) Round House Kick (4) Back Kick

Control Each Leg at hips minimum do control for 25 seconds without any support.

III. Sitting kicks with 1 kg Ankle Weight:

Do only 4 kicks (1) snap kicks (2) Side kick (3) Round house kick (4) Hook kick.
Do each kick 70 times alternative legs Lie down on back and wear 1kgs Ankle weight and kick continuously snap kicks for 70 kicks

Kneel led down and sit and hands support on the ground and raise your Right leg Right side and kick side kick continuously 30 kicks with wearing 1kg Ankle weights and change the leg and do with other leg same.

Kneel led down and sit and hands support on the ground and kick round house kick sideways 30 times each leg with wearing 1kgs Ankle weight.

Kneel led down and sit and hands support on the ground and kick Hook kick sideways 30 times each leg wearing 1kg Ankle weight

SPEED TRAINING OF PUNCHES - 13 TO 15 YEARS

Monday –I 4th week schedule

½ kg HAND WEIGHTS (Alternative Hands)

(a) Horse stand and hold ½ kg hand weight and Do 60 punches with alternative hands in 1 minute

(b) Stand in front forward stance and punch with single Right hand over the left open hand (Bend at elbow in the front) 20 punches with Single hand with ½ kg hand weight in 1 minute

And change the hand i.e. change to left hand and punch with the same as Right hand punch.

(C) Speed sitting hand weights punches Sit on chair or stool and punch at least 40 times with alternative hand (with left hand and right hand)

Variation: your can do this sitting punches by blind folded i.e. with closing eyes, by imagining you are smashing with punch.

(d) Forearm Exercise

Forearm and wrist strengthening

Stand with holding one sided dumbbell 8 pounds (approximately) sideways should be besides you and pull up as high as possible, Front side. Do with left hand and with right hand. This exercise will strengthen wrist, forearm.

(e) Forearm Strengthening Exercise

Stand with holding one sided dumbbell 8 pounds (approximately) with right hand beside your thigh and pull up and down back side 12 times each hand alternately.

(f) Wrist Strengthening Exercises

Sit on chair and hold one side dumbbell 8 pounds (approximately) with Right forearm on the thighs and twist to left and right side with maximum strain. Do with other hand, Do 10 times each.

(g) Forearm Strengthening

Sit on stool and holding bar with 15 pounds (approximately) weight with palm facing sky, as shown in picture with hands 10" inches apart and pull up your wrist to you and pull down 12 times. Note: Keep forearm and elbow on the thighs to balance the weight

(h) Forearm strengthening

Sit on stool and holding bar15 pounds (approximately) as shown in picture with hands 10" inches apart and pull to you and pull down 10 times. Note: Keep forearm and elbow on the thighs to balance the weight with palm facing floor in punching position

(i)Forearm Strengthening Exercises

Holding 12" to 15" long rod 8 pounds (approximately) tightly on the right side and twist 180degrees for 20 times and change the hand and continue.

Variations: You can hold 2 rods either side of each hand and twist them.

(j)Forearm Strengthening

Hold 12" to 14" rod 8 pounds (approximately) in front of you and twist left and right 180 degrees angle with left hand 18 repetitions and change to right hand and do the same repetitions.

(k) Triceps Strengthening Exercise

Keep index and thumb of each hand join together and go for pushups with leg stretch out without bending knees. Do this exercise for 10 times daily.

Friday: Same as on Monday Schedule

SPEED PEDDLE KICKS(kicking on pad)

Tuesday 4th week schedule

I. PAD KICKING EACH LEG 22 KICKS 1 TO 15 KICKS

(1) Push kick

(2) Front thrust kick

(3) Side kick

(4) Round house kick

(5) Back kick

(6) Outer edge kick

(7) Inner edge kick

(8) Down heel kick

(9) Hook kick

(10) Jumping side kick

(11) Jumping Round house kick

(12) Jumping Back kick

(13) Spin kick

(14) Jumping spin kick

(15) Scissor kick

II. PAD KICKING LEFT LEG 22KICKS IN 30 SECONDS SINGLE LEG

III. PAD KICKING RIGHT LEG 22 KICKS IN 30 SECONDS SINGLE LEG

Note: I,II and III Rest for 1 ½ minutes of each kick, Do all kicks accordingly

Thursday: Same as on Tuesday Schedule

SPEED NYLON / TUBE KICKING

Wednesday 4th week schedule

Speed Kicking With Tube

Tie bicycle tube or nylon thread and tie to your ankle and kick all kicks 22 times in 45 seconds alternative leg. Rest for 1 minute with each kick in air or kicking pad.
Do all kicks below mentioned stationary kicks 25 kicks in 45 seconds and 12 jumping kicks in 50 seconds.

Speed Kicking With Tube

Tie bicycle tube or nylon thread and tie to your ankle and kick all kicks 25 times with each leg.

This improves kicking speed. Once in a week you can do single leg kick and alternative leg kicks.

Do below mentioned kicks.

13. Side Kick with Left and Right Leg
14. Outer edge kick with Left and Right Leg
15. Inner edge kick with Left and Right Leg
16. Thrust kick with Left and Right Leg
17. Back kick with Left and Right Leg
18. Round house kick with Left and Right Leg
19. Hook Kick with Left and Right Leg
20. Jumping Round house kick with Left and Right Leg
21. Jumping side kick with Left and Right Leg
22. Down heel kick with Left and Right Leg
23. Jumping Thrust kick with Left and Right Leg
24. Jumping Back kick with Left and Right Leg

WEDNESDAY: <u>SPEED TRAINING OF PUNCHES</u>

4th week schedule

(i) Knuckle pushups, Close fist and keep knuckle on ground with shoulder width distance and go down and come up. Do 18 push ups and 70 punches in 1 minute.

(ii) Single hand knuckle pushups: Do one hand knuckle pushups 10 times one hand 20 punches in 1 minute and Change knuckles. Do alternate hands Do 2 sets

(iii) Power pushups for speed & power punches
Sit on kneeling position with palms facing ground and jump forward onto your palms on the Floor and Do 4 sets and get up and Do 150 punches in 2 minutes.

(iv) Pushing the kit bag and speed punch exercise: pushing the kit bag and 2 hands punches alternatively .Do 25 sets

Saturday: Tube kicking with single leg

4th week schedule

Tube kicking with single leg 25 kicks in 45 seconds one minute or 2 minutes Rest between each single leg kicks

Do all kicks 25 times in 45 seconds each leg. Below mentioned kicks.

1. Side Kick with Left and Right Leg
2. Hook Kick with Left and Right Leg
3. Outer edge kick with Left and Right Leg
4. Round house kick with Left and Right Leg
5. *Thrust kick* with Left and Right Leg
6. Back kick with Left and Right Leg
7. Jumping Round house kick with Left and Right Leg
8. Inner edge kick with Left and Right Leg

SPEED UNDER WATER KICKS & UNDER WATER PUNCHES

Sunday 4th week schedule, water workout (water must be chest level)

I. Under water kicks Do 1 to 8 kicks each leg 10 kicks (total 20 kicks) in 1 minute
Do below mentioned kicks

1.Inner edge kick

2.Thrust kick

3.Side kick

4.Spinning kick

5.Round house kick

6. Hook kick

7. Outer edge kick

8. Hook kick and side kick with holding wall

II. a. Running in the water :
Running in the water 20 meters

b. Side Running in the water :
Running in the water right side 20 meters and left side 20 meters

c. knee raising in the water :
Knee raising in the water each leg 40 times (Total 80 times)

d. punches in the water :
(i)100 double punches in the water with alternative hands
(ii)65 single hands punches with the left hand and right hand (Total 130 punches)

e. check the speed of every individual kicks in 1 minute and make a table of improvement (minimum kicks must be 150 kicks in 1 minute in Air every week)

SQUATS KICKS

Sunday Body Weight Squats Kicks below following kicks 4th week schedule

Sit on squat and get up and kick Down heel kick with one squat 2 kicks with the Right leg and left leg and sit. Do 10 kicks each leg (i.e. Total 20 kicks)

Sit on squat and get up and kick inner edge with Right leg and left leg and sit. Do 10 kicks each leg (i.e. Total 20kicks.

Sit on squat and get up and kick outer edge with left leg and Right leg and sit. Do 10 kicks each leg (i.e. Total 20 kicks).

Sit on squat and get up and kick front thrust kick with Right leg and with the Left leg and sit. Do 10 kicks each leg (i.e. Total 20 kicks) .

Sit on squat and get up and kick side kick with Right leg and with the Left leg and sit. Do 10 kicks each leg (i.e. Total 20 kicks).

Sit on squat and get up and kick front side kick with Right leg and with the Left leg and sit. Do 10 kicks each leg (i.e. Total 20 kicks).

Sit on squat and get up and kick Round house kick with Left leg and with the Right leg and sit. Do 10 kicks each leg (i.e. Total 20 kicks).

Sit on squat and get up and kick Back kick with Right leg and with the Left leg and sit. Do 10 kicks each leg (i.e. Total 20 kicks).

Sit on squat and get up and kick Hook kick with Left leg and with the Right leg and sit. Do 10 kicks each leg (i.e. Total 20 kicks).

SPEED TRAINING OF KICKS - BELOW 13 YEARS

Monday –I 4th & 5th week schedule

90 KICKS IN 2 MINITUES

Each kick you need to do a minimum of 45 kicks each leg in 1 minute Rest for 2 minute. Do all 1 to 10 kicks. Below mention kicks

1. down heel kick, alternative legs
2. Side Kick, alternative Legs
3. Spinning cart wheel kick, alternative legs
4. Hook Kick, alternative Legs
5. Trust Kick alternative Leg
6. Inner edge kicks alternative legs
7. Front side kicks alternative legs
8. Round House Kick Alternative Legs
9. Outer Edge Kick Alternative Legs
10. Back Kick and Do Alternative Leg

II. Kick Controlling:

Do only 4 Kicks i.e., (1) Thrust Kick (2) Side Kick (3) Round House Kick (4) Back Kick

Control Each Leg at hips minimum do control for 25 to 30 seconds without any support.

III. Sitting kicks:

Do only 4 kicks (1) snap kicks (2) Side kick (3) Round house kick (4) Hook kick. Do each kick 70 times alternative legs Lie down on back and kick continuously snap kicks start from 35 kicks to 70 kicks

Kneel led down and sit and hands support on the ground and raise your Right leg Right side and kick side kick continuously 35 to 70 and change the leg and do with other leg same.

Kneel led down and sit and hands support on the ground and kick round house kick sideways 35 to 70 times each leg.

Kneel led down and sit and hands support on the ground and kick Hook kick sideways 35 to 70 times each leg.

Variation: kicks on x-ray film. You can do all kicks and all punches on x-ray film each kick 15 times and 75 punch with 2 hands.

SPEED TRAINING OF PUNCHES - BELOW 13 YEARS

Monday –I 4th & 5th week schedule

140 punches in 1 minute (Alternative Hands)

(a) Horse stand and Do 140 punches with alternative hands in 1 minute Do 2 sets.

(b) Stand in front forward stance and punch with single Right hand over the left open hand (Bend at elbow in the front) 75 punches with Single hand with in 1 minute Do 2 sets And change the hand i.e. change to left hand and punch with the same as Right hand punch.

(c) Speed sitting hand punches Sit on chair or stool and punch at least 100 times with alternative hand (with left hand and right hand) Do 2 sets.
Variation: your can do this sitting punches by blind folded i.e. with closing eyes, by imagining you are smashing with punch.

(d) Punches on x-ray film: you can practices 75 with each hand (total 150 punches)

(e) Triceps Strengthening Exercise
Keep index and thumb of each hand join together and go for pushups with leg stretch out without bending knees. Do this exercise for 10 to 12 times daily.

Friday: Same as on Monday Schedule

SPEED PEDDLE KICKS(kicking on pad)

Tuesday 4th &5th week schedule

I. PAD KICKING EACH LEG 25 KICKS 1 TO 15 KICKS

(1) Push kick - 25 kicks each leg
(2) Front thrust kick " "
(3) Side kick " "
(4) Round house kick " "
(5) Back kick " "
(6) Outer edge kick " "
(7) Inner edge kick " "
(8) Down heel kick " "
(9) Hook kick " "
(10) Jumping side kick " "
(11) Jumping Round house kick " "

(12) Jumping Back kick - 20 kicks each leg

(13) Spin kick -25 kicks each leg

(14) Jumping spin kick -20 kicks each leg

(15) Scissor kick - 25 kicks each leg

II. PAD KICKING LEFT LEG 25 KICKS IN 1MINITE SINGLE LEG

III. PAD KICKING RIGHT LEG 25 KICKS IN 1MINITE SINGLE LEG

Note: I,II and III Rest for 1 ½ minutes of each kick, Do all kicks accordingly

Thursday: Same as on Tuesday Schedule

WEDNESDAY: SPEED TRAINING OF PUNCHES

4th & 5th week schedule

(i) Knuckle pushups, Close fist and keep knuckle on ground with shoulder width distance and go down and come up or palms pushups Do 12 pushups and 75 punches in 1 minute.

(ii) Single hand knuckle or palms pushups: Do one hand knuckle pushups 12 times one hand 40 punches in 1 minute and Change knuckles. Do alternate hands Do 2 sets

(iii) Power pushups for speed & power punches
Sit on kneeling position with palms facing ground and jump forward onto your palms on the Floor and Do 3 sets and get up and Do 150 punches in 3 minutes.

(iv) Pushing the kit bag and speed punch exercise: pushing the kit bag and 2 hands punches alternatively .Do 25 sets

SPEED UNDER WATER KICKS & UNDER WATER PUNCHES

Sunday 4th & 5th week schedule, water workout (water must be chest level)

III. Under water kicks Do 1 to 8 kicks each leg 10 kicks (total 20 kicks) in 1 minute Do below mentioned kicks

1.Inner edge kick

2.Thrust kick

3.Side kick

4.Spinning kick

5.Round house kick

6. Hook kick

7. Outer edge kick

8. Hook kick and side kick with holding wall

II. a. Running in the water :
Running in the water 12 meters

b. Side Running in the water :
Running in the water right side 12 meters and left side 12 meters

c. knee raising in the water :
Knee raising in the water each leg 30 times (Total 60 times)

d. punches in the water :
(i) 75 double punches in the water with alternative hands
(ii)50 single hands punches with the left hand and right hand (Total 100 punches)

e. check every week the speed of every individual kicks in 1 minute and make a table of improvement (minimum kicks must be 140 kicks in 1 minute in Air every week)

SQUATS KICKS

Sunday Body Weight Squats Kicks below following kicks
4th & 5th week schedule

Sit on squat and get up and kick Down heel kick with one squat 2 kicks with the Right leg and left leg and sit. Do 10 kicks each leg (i.e. Total 20 kicks) in 1 minute.

Sit on squat and get up and kick inner edge with Right leg and left leg and sit. Do 10 kicks each leg (i.e. Total 20 kicks) in 1 minute.
Sit on squat and get up and kick outer edge with left leg and Right leg and sit. Do 10 kicks each leg (i.e. Total 20 kicks) in 1 minute.

Sit on squat and get up and kick front thrust kick with Right leg and with the Left leg and sit. Do 10 kicks each leg (i.e. Total 20 kicks) in 1 minute.

Sit on squat and get up and kick side kick with Right leg and with the Left leg and sit. Do 10 kicks each leg (i.e. Total 20 kicks) in 1 minute.

Sit on squat and get up and kick front side kick with Right leg and with the Left leg and sit. Do 10 kicks each leg (i.e. Total 20 kicks) in 1 minute.

Sit on squat and get up and kick Round house kick with Left leg and with the Right leg and sit. Do 10 kicks each leg (i.e. Total 20 kicks) in 1 minute.

Sit on squat and get up and kick Back kick with Right leg and with the Left leg and sit. Do 10 kicks each leg (i.e. Total 20 kicks) in 1 minute.

Sit on squat and get up and kick Hook kick with Left leg and with the Right leg and sit. Do 10 kicks each leg (i.e. Total 20 kicks) in 1 minute.

5[Th] Week

Speed Training schedule for 15 Years and above

Speed Training schedule for 13 – 15 Years

Speed Training schedule for below 13 years

"Practicing daily improves in the beginning, improved practice makes progress"

\- Grand Master M. Jayanth Reddy

SPEED TRAINING OF KICKS- 15 YEAR AND ABOVE

Monday –I   5th week schedule

1 ½ kgs ANKLE (LEG) WEIGHTS KICKS(Alternative Legs)

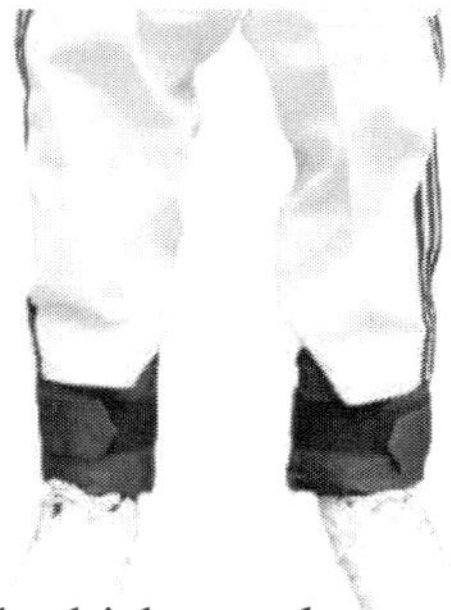

Wear an Ankle weight to your leg 1 ½ kg each leg and start kicking all the kicks as shown in the pictures below. Each kick you need to do a minimum of 35 kicks each leg in 1 minute each Rest for 2 minute. Do all 1 to 10 kicks.

1.DOWN HEEL KICK, ALTERNATIVE LEGS

2.SIDE KICK, ALTERNATIVE LEGS

3.SPINNING CART WHEEL KICK, ALTERNATIVE LEGS

4.HOOK KICK, ALTERNATIVE LEGS

5.TRUST KICK ALTENATIVE LEG

6. INNER EDGE KICKS ALTERNATIVE LEGS

7. FRONT SIDE KICKS ALTERNATIVE LEGS

8. ROUND HOUSE KICK ALTERNATIVE LEGS

9. OUTER EDGE KICK ALTERNATIVE LEGS

10. BACK KICK AND DO ALTERNATIVE LEG

II. 1 ½ kgs of Ankle Weight kick Controlling:

Do only 4 Kicks i.e., (1) Thrust Kick (2) Side Kick (3) Round House Kick (4) Back Kick Control Each Leg at hips minimum do control for 20 to 25 seconds without any support. See Picture A,B,C and D, Do 2 sets each.

Pic-A

Thrust Kick, Alternative Legs

Pic-B

Side Kick, Alternative

Pic-C

Round House Kick Alternative

Pic-D

Back Kick do with Alternative Leg

III. Sitting kicks with 1 ½ kegs Ankle Weight:

Do only 4 kicks (1) snap kicks (2) Side kick (3) Round house kick (4) Hook kick.
Do each kick 90 times alternative legs Lie down on back and wear 1 ½ kgs Ankle weight and kick continuously snap kicks for 45 to 60 kicks see pic-P1 ,pic- P2 and p3.

Pic-P1

Pic-P2

Pic-P3

Kneel led down and sit and hands support on the ground and raise your Right leg Right side and kick side kick continuously 45 to 60 kicks with wearing 1 ½ kg Ankle weights and change the leg and do with other leg same. See pic-P4 and pic-P5.

pic-P4

pic-P5

Kneel led down and sit and hands support on the ground and kick round house kick sideways 45 to 60 times each leg with wearing 1 ½ kgs Ankle weight. See pic-P6 and pic-P7

pic-P6

pic-P7

Kneel led down and sit and hands support on the ground and kick Hook kick sideways 45 to 60 times each leg wearing 1 ½ kgs Ankle weight. See pic-P8 and pic-P9.

pic-P8

pic-P9

SPEED TRAINING OF PUNCHES - 15 YEAR AND ABOVE

Monday –I 5th week schedule

1kgs HAND WEIGHTS (Alternative Hands)

(a) Horse stand Horse stand and hold 1 kg hand weight and Do 100 punches with alternative hands with 1kg hand weight in 1 minute See picture 1 and 2

Pic -1

Pic -2

(b) Stand in front forward stance and punch with single Right hand over the left open hand (Bend at elbow in the front) 50 punches with Single hand with 1kg hand weight in 1 minute

And change the hand i.e. change to left hand And punch with the same as Right hand punch.

See picture 3,4,5 and 6

Pic -3

Pic -4

Pic -5

Pic -6

(c) Speed sitting hand weights punches Sit on chair or stool and punch at least 80 times with alternative hand (with left hand and right hand)

Variation: your can do this sitting punches by blind folded i.e. with closing eyes, by imagining you are smashing with punch. See picture 7 and 8

Pic -7

Pic -8

D) Biceps Forearm Triceps Strengthening Exercises for Speed

Bicep Exercise 1

Hold 10 pounds in left hand and pull till chest. This will strengthen the biceps. Do with other hand each 2 sets of 15 times. Refer pictures A, B , A1 and B1

Pic -A

Pic -B

Pic -A1

Pic - B1

Bicep Exercise 2

Sit on chair and take 10 pounds hand dumbbell and pull up to chest level 15 repetitions each hand alternatively. Refer pictures A, B, C and D

Pic -A

Pic -B

Pic -B

Pic -D

Triceps Strengthening 3

Horse stance with barbell weight back of you and slightly bend forward your upper body and lift weight 15 pounds. See picture A.

Pic - A

Biceps Strengthening 4

Stand with barbell weight on your hand forward pull weight up to chest and withdraw to thighs. Do with 15 pounds increases according to your capacity. Do at least 15 repetitions Do 2 sets. . See picture A.

Pic -A

Forearm Exercise 5

Forearm and wrist strengthening

Stand with holding one sided dumbbell 8 pounds (approximately) sideways should be besides you and pull up as high as possible, Front side. Do with left hand and with right hand. This exercise will strengthen wrist, forearm. See pictures A, B, A1 and B1.

Pic - A Pic - B Pic – A1 Pic – B1

Forearm Strengthening Exercise 6

Stand with holding one sided dumbbell 8 pounds (approximately) with right hand beside your thigh and pull up and down back side 15 times each hand alternately. See picture C and D.

Pic - C

Pic - D

Wrist Strengthening Exercises7

Sit on chair and hold one side dumbbell 8 pounds (approximately) with Right forearm on the thighs and twist to left and right side with maximum strain. Do with other hand, Do 10 times each. See pictures A, B, C, D, E, and F

Pic -A

Pic - B

Pic - C

Pic -D

Pic - E

Pic - F

Triceps Exercise 8

Sit on chair and hold one side Drum bell 8 to 10 pounds (approximately) with Right hand Back side and pull up and Down, See pictures S1, S2, S3, and S4

Pic – S1

Pic – S2

Pic – S3

Pic – S4

Forearm Strengthening 9

Sit on stool and holding bar with 15 pounds (approximately) weight with palm facing sky, as shown in picture with hands 10" inches apart and pull up your wrist to you and pull down 15 times. Note: Keep forearm and elbow on the thighs to balance the weight. See pictures A and B.

Pic – A

Pic - B

Forearm strengthening 10

Sit on stool and holding bar15 pounds (approximately) as shown in picture with hands 10" inches apart and pull to you and pull down 15 times. Note: Keep forearm and elbow on the thighs to balance the weight with palm facing floor in punching position. See pictures C and D.

Pic – C

Pic – D

Forearm Strengthening Exercises 11

Holding 12" to 15" long rod 8 pounds (approximately) tightly on the right side and twist 180degrees for 20 times and change the hand and continue. See pictures A, B, C

Variations: You can hold 2 rods either side of each hand and twist them.

Pic - A

Pic - B

Pic - C

Forearm Strengthening 12

Hold 12" to 14" rod 8 pounds (approximately) in front of you and twist left and right 180 degrees angle with left hand 20 repetitions and change to right hand and do the same repetitions. See pictures A, B, C, D, E and F.

Pic - A

Pic – B

Pic – C

Pic- D

Pic – E

Pic - F

Triceps Strengthening Exercise 13

Keep index and thumb of each hand join together and go for pushups with leg stretch out without bending knees. Do this exercise for 10 to 15 times daily. See pictures A and B.

Pic - A

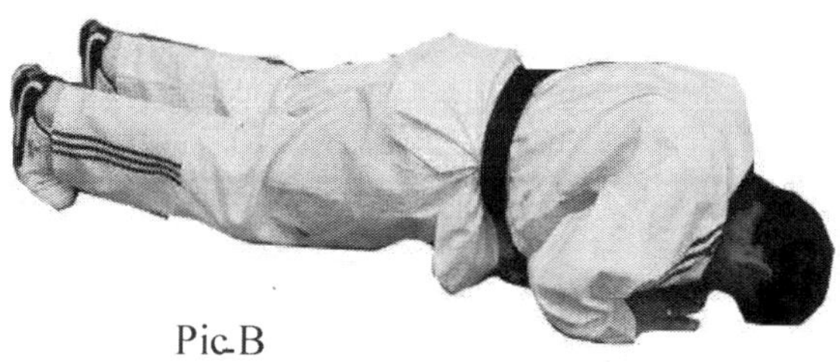

Pic-B

Friday: Same as on Monday Schedule

SPEED PEDDLE KICKS(kicking on pad)

Tuesday 5th week schedule

I. PAD KICKING EACH LEG 35 KICKS 1 TO 15 KICKS

(1) Push kick

(2) Front thrust kick

(3) Side kick

(4) Round house kick

(5) Back kick

(6) Outer edge kick

(7) Inner edge kick

(8) Down heel kick

(9) Hook kick

(10) Jumping side kick

(11) Jumping Round house kick

(12) Jumping Back kick

(13) Spin kick

(14) Jumping spin kick

(15) Scissor kick

Jumping thrust kick

Push Kick on Pad -1

Front thrust kick on pad -2

Side kick on pad -3

Round house on pad-4

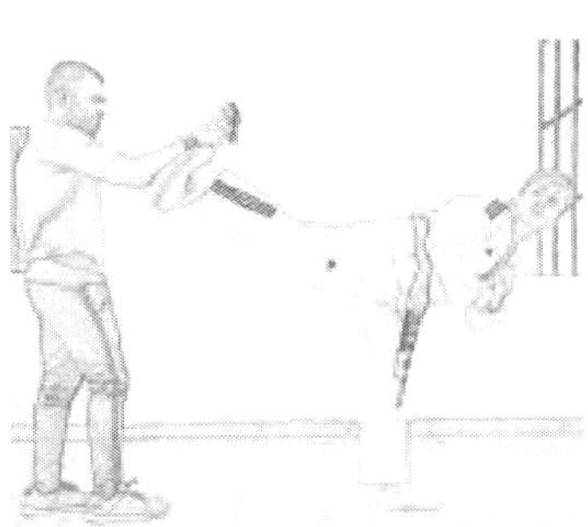

Back kick on pad -5

Outer edge kick on pad – 6

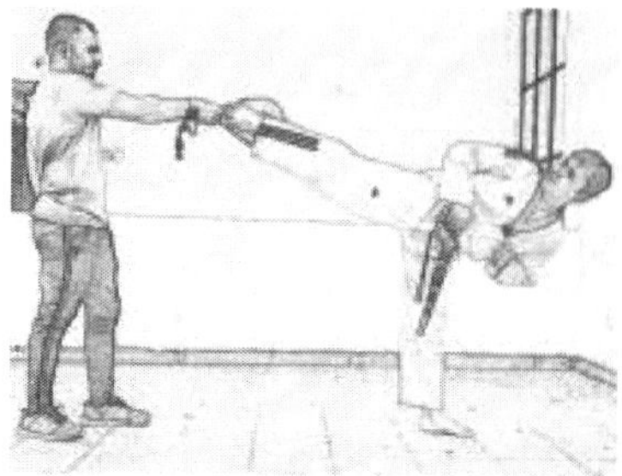

Inner edge kick on pad -7 Down heel kick on pad -8 Hook kick on pad – 9

Jumping side kick on pad – 10 Jumping Round house kick on pad - 11 Jumping Back kick on pad – 12

Jumping spin kick on pad - 13 Front Side kick -14 Scissor kick-15

II. PAD KICKING LEFT LEG 30 KICKS IN 30 SECONDS SINGLE LEG

III. PAD KICKING RIGHT LEG 30 KICKS IN 30 SECONDS SINGLE LEG

Note: I,II and III Rest for 1 ½ minutes of each kick, Do all kicks accordingly

Thursday: Same as on Tuesday Schedule

SPEED NYLON / TUBE KICKING

Wednesday 5th week schedule

Speed Kicking With Tube

Tie bicycle tube or nylon thread and tie to your ankle and kick all kicks 30 times in 45 seconds alternative leg. Rest for 1 minute with each kick.
Do all kicks below mentioned stationary kicks 30 kicks in 45 seconds and 15 jumping kicks in 50 seconds.

Speed Kicking With Tube

Tie bicycle tube or nylon thread and tie to your ankle and kick all kicks 30 times with each leg.
This improves kicking speed. Once in a week you can do single leg kick and alternative leg kicks.

Side Kick with Left

Side Kick with Right

Hook

Outer edge kick

Round house kick

Thrust kick

Back kick

Back kick

Jumping Round house kick

Jumping side kick with Right leg

Jumping side kick with Left leg

SPEED KICKING ON PAD WITH TIEING TUBE

Down heel kick with tube

Inner edge kick with tube

Outer edge kick with tube

Front thrust kick with tube

Round house kick with tube

Side kick with tube

Back kick with tube

Hook kick with tube

Jumping Round house kick with tube

Jumping Back kick with tube

Jumping side kick with tube

Jumping thrust kick with tube

Turning Jumping Round house
kick with tube Pic -A1

Turning Jumping Round house
kick with tube pic-A2

Turning Jumping Round house kick
with tube Pic -A3

WEDNESDAY: **SPEED TRAINING OF PUNCHES**

5th week schedule

(v) Knuckle pushups, Close fist and keep knuckle on ground with shoulder width distance and go down and come up. Do 25 pushups and 125 punches in 1 minute. See pictures A and B and C

Pic - A

Pic- C

Pic - B

(ii) Single hand knuckle pushups: Do one hand knuckle pushups 12 times one hand 35 punches in 1 minute and Change knuckles. Do alternate hands Do 2 sets. See picture A

Pic - A

(iii) Power pushups for speed & power punches

Sit on kneeling position with palms facing ground and jump forward onto your palms on the floor as shown in pictures A and B. Do 5 sets and get up and Do 175 punches in 3 minutes.

Pic A

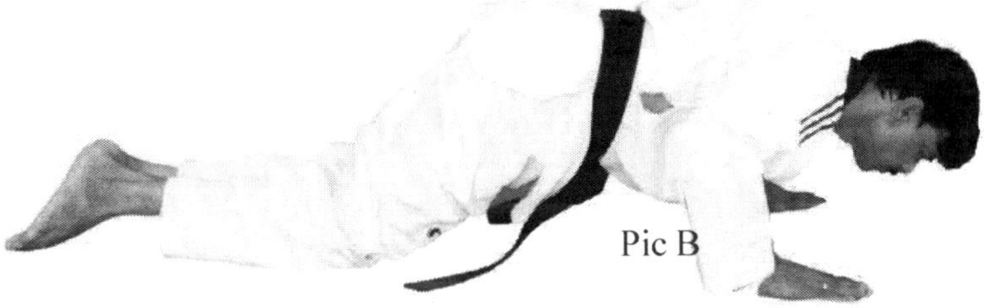

Pic B

(iv)) Pushing the kit bag and speed punch exercise: pushing the kit bag and 2 hands punches alternatively .Do 35 sets See pic- P1, P2 and P3

Pic –P1

Pic –P2

Pic –P3

Saturday: Tube kicking with single leg

5th week schedule

Tube kicking with single leg 35 kicks in 45 seconds one minute Rest between each single leg kicks

Do all kicks 35 times in 45 seconds each leg. Below mentioned kicks.

Side Kick with Left

Side Kick with Right

Hook

Outer edge kick

Round house kick

Thrust kick

Back kick

Back kick

Jumping Round house kick

SPEED UNDER WATER KICKS & UNDER WATER PUNCHES

Sunday 5th week schedule, water workout (water must be chest level)

I. Under water kicks Do 1 to 8 kicks each leg 12 kicks (total 24 kicks) in 1 minute

1.Inner edge kick

2.Thrust kick

3.Side kick

4.Spinning kick

5.Round house kick

6. Hook kick

7. Outer edge kick

8. Hook kick and side kick with holding wall

II. a. Running in the water :
Running in the water 25 meters

b. Side Running in the water :
Running in the water right side 25 meters and left side 25 meters

c. knee raising in the water :
Knee raising in the water each leg 50 times (Total 100 times)

d. punches in the water :
(i)125 double punches in the water with alternative hands
(ii)90 single hands punches with the left hand and right hand (Total 180 punches)

e. check the speed of every individual kicks in 1 minute and make a of table improvement (minimum kicks must be 140 kicks in 1 minute)

f. check the speed of every individual kicks in 1 minute and make a of table improvement

SQUATS KICKS

Sunday Body Weight Squats Kicks below following kicks

5th week schedule

Sit on squat and get up and kick Down heel kick with one squat 2 kicks the Right leg and left leg and sit. Do 12 kicks each leg (i.e. Total 24 kicks) See pic-L1,pic-L2,pic-L3 and pic-4

Pic-L1

Pic-L2

Pic-L3

Pic-L4

Sit on squat and get up and kick inner edge with Right leg and left leg and sit. Do 12 kicks each leg (i.e. Total 24 kicks) see pic- L5 and pic-L6.

Sit on squat and get up and kick outer edge with left leg and Right leg and sit. Do 12 kicks each leg (i.e. Total 24 kicks) See pic- L7 and pic-L8.

Sit on squat and get up and kick front thrust kick with Right leg and with the Left leg and sit. Do 12 kicks each leg (i.e. Total 24 kicks) See pic-L9 and pic-L10

Pic-L5

Pic-L6

Pic-L7

Pic-L8

Pic-L9

Pic-L10

Sit on squat and get up and kick side kick with Right leg and with the Left leg and sit. Do 12 kicks each leg (i.e. Total 24 kicks) See pic-L11 and pic-L12.

Sit on squat and get up and kick front side kick with Right leg and with the Left leg and sit. Do 12 kicks each leg (i.e. Total 24 kicks) See pic-L13 and pic-L14.

Sit on squat and get up and kick Round house kick with Left leg and with the Right leg and sit. Do 12 kicks each leg (i.e. Total 24 kicks) See pic-L15 and pic-L16.

Pic-L11

Pic-L12

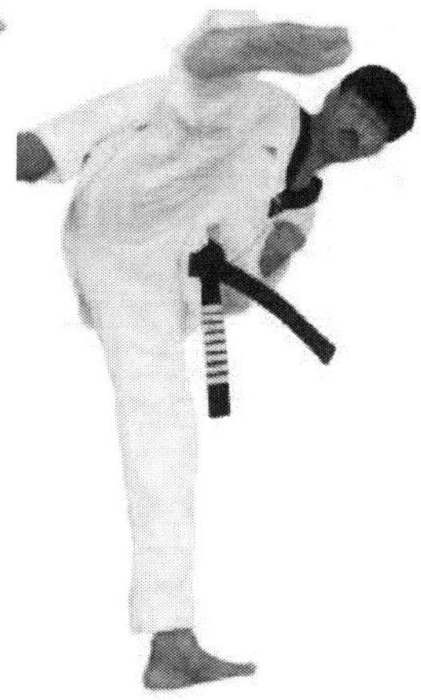

Pic-L13

Pic-L14

Pic-L15

Pic-L16 (side view)

Sit on squat and get up and kick Back kick with Right leg and with the Left leg and sit. Do 12 kicks each leg (i.e. Total 24 kicks) See pic-L17,pic-L18 and L19 Back kick in Front View.

Pic-L17

Pic-L18

Back kick Front view Pic-L19

Sit on squat and get up and kick Hook kick with Left leg and with the Right leg and sit. Do 12 kicks each leg (i.e. Total 24 kicks) See pic-L20,pic-L21 Front view.

Pic-L20 (Side View)

Hook kick front viewPic-L21

SPEED TRAINING OF KICKS-13 TO 15 YEARS

Monday –I 5th week schedule

1kg ANKLE (LEG) WEIGHTS KICKS(Alternative Legs)

Wear a Ankle weight to your leg 1 kg each leg and start kicking all the kicks as shown in the pictures below. Each kick you need to do a minimum of 45 kicks each leg in 1 minute Rest for 2 minute. Do all 1 to 10 kicks.

1. down heel kick, alternative legs
2. Side Kick, alternative Legs
3. Spinning cart wheel kick, alternative legs
4. Hook Kick, alternative Legs
5. Trust Kick alternative Leg
6. Inner edge kicks alternative legs
7. Front side kicks alternative legs
8. Round House Kick Alternative Legs
9. Outer Edge Kick Alternative Legs
10. Back Kick and Do Alternative Leg

II. 1kgs of Ankle Weight kick Controlling:

Do only 4 Kicks i.e., (1) Thrust Kick (2) Side Kick (3) Round House Kick (4) Back Kick

Control Each Leg at hips minimum do control for 25 seconds without any support.

III. Sitting kicks with 1 kg Ankle Weight:

Do only 4 kicks (1) snap kicks (2) Side kick (3) Round house kick (4) Hook kick.
Do each kick 75 times alternative legs Lie down on back and wear 1kgs Ankle weight and kick continuously snap kicks for 75 kicks

Kneel Led down and sit and hands support on the ground and raise your Right leg Right side and kick side kick continuously 35 kicks with wearing 1kg Ankle weights and change the leg and do with other leg same.

Kneel down and sit and hands support on the ground and kick round house kick sideways 35 times each leg with wearing 1kgs Ankle weight.

Kneel down and sit and hands support on the ground and kick Hook kick sideways 35 times each leg wearing 1kg Ankle weight

SPEED TRAINING OF PUNCHES - 13 TO 15 YEARS

Monday –I 5th week schedule

½ kg HAND WEIGHTS (Alternative Hands)

(a) Horse stand and hold ½ kg hand weight and Do 65 punches with alternative hands in 1 minute

(b) Stand in front forward stance and punch with single Right hand over the left open hand (Bend at elbow in the front) 25 punches with Single hand with ½ kg hand weight in 1 minute
And change the hand i.e. change to left hand and punch with the same as Right hand punch.

(C) Speed sitting hand weights punches Sit on chair or stool and punch at least 45 times with alternative hand (with left hand and right hand)
Variation: your can do this sitting punches by blind folded i.e. with closing eyes, by imagining you are smashing with punch.

(d) Forearm Exercise
Forearm and wrist strengthening
Stand with holding one sided dumbbell 8 pounds (approximately) sideways should be besides you and pull up as high as possible, Front side. Do with left hand and with right hand. This exercise will strengthen wrist, forearm.

(e) Forearm Strengthening Exercise
Stand with holding one sided dumbbell 8 pounds (approximately) with right hand beside your thigh and pull up and down back side 13 times each hand alternately.

(f) Wrist Strengthening Exercises
Sit on chair and hold one side dumbbell 8 pounds (approximately) with Right forearm on the thighs and twist to left and right side with maximum strain. Do with other hand, Do 10 times each.

(g) Forearm Strengthening
Sit on stool and holding bar with 15 pounds (approximately) weight with palm facing sky, as shown in picture with hands 10" inches apart and pull up your wrist to you and pull down 14 times. Note: Keep forearm and elbow on the thighs to balance the weight

(h) Forearm strengthening
Sit on stool and holding bar15 pounds (approximately) as shown in picture with hands 10" inches apart and pull to you and pull down 10 times. Note: Keep forearm and elbow on the thighs to balance the weight with palm facing floor in punching position

(i)Forearm Strengthening Exercises
Holding 12" to 15" long rod 8 pounds (approximately) tightly on the right side and twist 180degrees for 20 times and change the hand and continue.
Variations: You can hold 2 rods either side of each hand and twist them.

(j)Forearm Strengthening

Hold 12" to 14" rod 8 pounds (approximately) in front of you and twist left and right 180 degrees angle with left hand 18 repetitions and change to right hand and do the same repetitions.

(k) Triceps Strengthening Exercise

Keep index and thumb of each hand join together and go for pushups with leg stretch out without bending knees. Do this exercise for 10 times daily.

Friday: Same as on Monday Schedule

SPEED PEDDLE KICKS(kicking on pad)

Tuesday 5th week schedule

I. PAD KICKING EACH LEG 25 KICKS 1 TO 15 KICKS

(1) Push kick

(2) Front thrust kick

(3) Side kick

(4) Round house kick

(5) Back kick

(6) Outer edge kick

(7) Inner edge kick

(8) Down heel kick

(9) Hook kick

(10) Jumping side kick

(11) Jumping Round house kick

(12) Jumping Back kick

(13) Spin kick

(14) Jumping spin kick

(15) Scissor kick

II. PAD KICKING LEFT LEG 25KICKS IN 30 SECONDS SINGLE LEG

III. PAD KICKING RIGHT LEG 25 KICKS IN 30 SECONDS SINGLE LEG

Note: I,II and III Rest for 1 ½ minutes of each kick, Do all kicks accordingly

Thursday: Same as on Tuesday Schedule

SPEED NYLON / TUBE KICKING

Wednesday 5th week schedule

Speed Kicking With Tube

Tie bicycle tube or nylon thread and tie to your ankle and kick all kicks 25 times in 45 seconds alternative leg. Rest for 1 minute with each kick in air or kicking pad.
Do all kicks below mentioned stationary kicks 30 kicks in 45 seconds and 14 jumping kicks in 50 seconds.

Speed Kicking With Tube

Tie bicycle tube or nylon thread and tie to your ankle and kick all kicks 30 times with each leg.

This improves kicking speed. Once in a week you can do single leg kick and alternative leg kicks.

Do below mentioned kicks.

1. Side Kick with Left and Right Leg
2. Outer edge kick with Left and Right Leg
3. Inner edge kick with Left and Right Leg
4. Thrust kick with Left and Right Leg
5. Back kick with Left and Right Leg
6. Round house kick with Left and Right Leg
7. Hook Kick with Left and Right Leg
8. Jumping Round house kick with Left and Right Leg
9. Jumping side kick with Left and Right Leg
10. Down heel kick with Left and Right Leg
11. Jumping Thrust kick with Left and Right Leg
12. Jumping Back kick with Left and Right Leg

WEDNESDAY: SPEED TRAINING OF PUNCHES

5th week schedule

(i) Knuckle pushups, Close fist and keep knuckle on ground with shoulder width distance and go down and come up. Do 20 push ups and 75 punches in 1 minute.

(ii) Single hand knuckle pushups: Do one hand knuckle pushups 10 times one hand 20 punches in 1 minute and Change knuckles. Do alternate hands Do 2 sets

(iii) Power pushups for speed & power punches
Sit on kneeling position with palms facing ground and jump forward onto your palms on the Floor and Do 4 sets and get up and Do 160 punches in 2 minutes.

(iv) Pushing the kit bag and speed punch exercise: pushing the kit bag and 2 hands punches alternatively .Do 30 sets

Saturday: Tube kicking with single leg

5th week schedule

Tube kicking with single leg 30 kicks in 45 seconds one minute or 2 minutes Rest between each single leg kicks

Do all kicks 30 times in 45 seconds each leg. Below mentioned kicks.

1. Side Kick with Left and Right Leg
2. Hook Kick with Left and Right Leg
3. Outer edge kick with Left and Right Leg
4. Round house kick with Left and Right Leg
5. *Thrust kick* with Left and Right Leg
6. Back kick with Left and Right Leg
7. Jumping Round house kick with Left and Right Leg
8. Inner edge kick with Left and Right Leg

SPEED UNDER WATER KICKS & UNDER WATER PUNCHES

Sunday 5th week schedule, water workout (water must be chest level)

I. Under water kicks Do 1 to 8 kicks each leg 11 kicks (total 22 kicks) in 1 minute
Do below mentioned kicks

1.Inner edge kick

2.Thrust kick

3.Side kick

4.Spinning kick

5.Round house kick

6. Hook kick

7. Outer edge kick

8. Hook kick and side kick with holding wall

II. a. Running in the water :
Running in the water 20 meters

b. Side Running in the water :
Running in the water right side 20 meters and left side 20 meters

c. knee raising in the water :
Knee raising in the water each leg 40 times (Total 80 times)

d. punches in the water :
(i)115 double punches in the water with alternative hands
(ii)75 single hands punches with the left hand and right hand (Total 150 punches)

e. check the speed of every individual kicks in 1 minute and make a table of improvement (minimum kicks must be 160 kicks in 1 minute in Air every week)

SQUATS KICKS

Sunday Body Weight Squats Kicks below following kicks 5th week schedule

Sit on squat and get up and kick Down heel kick with one squat 2 kicks with the Right leg and left leg and sit. Do 12 kicks each leg (i.e. Total 24 kicks)

Sit on squat and get up and kick inner edge with Right leg and left leg and sit. Do 12 kicks each leg (i.e. Total 24kicks.

Sit on squat and get up and kick outer edge with left leg and Right leg and sit. Do 12 kicks each leg (i.e. Total 24 kicks).

Sit on squat and get up and kick front thrust kick with Right leg and with the Left leg and sit. Do 12 kicks each leg (i.e. Total 24 kicks) .

Sit on squat and get up and kick side kick with Right leg and with the Left leg and sit. Do 12 kicks each leg (i.e. Total 24 kicks).

Sit on squat and get up and kick front side kick with Right leg and with the Left leg and sit. Do 12 kicks each leg (i.e. Total 24 kicks).

Sit on squat and get up and kick Round house kick with Left leg and with the Right leg and sit. Do 12 kicks each leg (i.e. Total 24 kicks).

Sit on squat and get up and kick Back kick with Right leg and with the Left leg and sit. Do 12 kicks each leg (i.e. Total 24 kicks).

Sit on squat and get up and kick Hook kick with Left leg and with the Right leg and sit. Do 12 kicks each leg (i.e. Total 24 kicks).

SPEED TRAINING OF KICKS - BELOW 13 YEARS

Monday –I 4th & 5th week schedule

90 KICKS IN 2 MINITUES

Each kick you need to do a minimum of 45 kicks each leg in 1 minute Rest for 2 minute. Do all 1 to 10 kicks. Below mention kicks

1. down heel kick, alternative legs
2. Side Kick, alternative Legs
3. Spinning cart wheel kick, alternative legs
4. Hook Kick, alternative Legs
5. Trust Kick alternative Leg
6. Inner edge kicks alternative legs
7. Front side kicks alternative legs
8. Round House Kick Alternative Legs
9. Outer Edge Kick Alternative Legs
10. Back Kick and Do Alternative Leg

II. Kick Controlling:

Do only 4 Kicks i.e., (1) Thrust Kick (2) Side Kick (3) Round House Kick (4) Back Kick

Control Each Leg at hips minimum do control for 25 to 30 seconds without any support.

III. Sitting kicks:

Do only 4 kicks (1) snap kicks (2) Side kick (3) Round house kick (4) Hook kick.
Do each kick 70 times alternative legs Lie down on back and kick continuously snap kicks start from 35 kicks to 70 kicks

Kneel Led down and sit and hands support on the ground and raise your Right leg Right side and kick side kick continuously 35 to 70 and change the leg and do with other leg same.

Kneel down and sit and hands support on the ground and kick round house kick sideways 35 to 70 times each leg.

Kneel down and sit and hands support on the ground and kick Hook kick sideways 35 to 70 times each leg.

Variation: kicks on x-ray film. You can do all kicks and all punches on x-ray film each kick 15 times and 75 punch with 2 hands.

SPEED TRAINING OF PUNCHES - BELOW 13 YEARS

Monday –I $4^{th \& 5th}$ week schedule

140 punches in 1 minute (Alternative Hands)

(a) Horse stand and Do 140 punches with alternative hands in 1 minute Do 2 sets.

(b) Stand in front forward stance and punch with single Right hand over the left open hand (Bend at elbow in the front) 75 punches with Single hand with in 1 minute Do 2 sets And change the hand i.e. change to left hand and punch with the same as Right hand punch.

(C) Speed sitting hand punches Sit on chair or stool and punch at least 100 times with alternative hand (with left hand and right hand) Do 2 sets.
Variation: your can do this sitting punches by blind folded i.e. with closing eyes, by imagining you are smashing with punch.

(d) Punches on x-ray film: you can practices 75 with each hand (total 150 punches)

(e) Triceps Strengthening Exercise
Keep index and thumb of each hand join together and go for pushups with leg stretch out without bending knees. Do this exercise for 10 to 12 times daily.

Friday: Same as on Monday Schedule

SPEED PEDDLE KICKS(kicking on pad)

Tuesday $4^{th \& 5th}$ week schedule

I. PAD KICKING EACH LEG 25 KICKS 1 TO 15 KICKS

(1) Push kick - 25 kicks each leg
(2) Front thrust kick " "
(3) Side kick " "
(4) Round house kick " "
(5) Back kick " "
(6) Outer edge kick " "
(7) Inner edge kick " "
(8) Down heel kick " "
(9) Hook kick " "
(10) Jumping side kick " "
(11) Jumping Round house kick " "

(12) Jumping Back kick - 20 kicks each leg

(13) Spin kick -25 kicks each leg

(14) Jumping spin kick -20 kicks each leg

(15) Scissor kick - 25 kicks each leg

II. PAD KICKING LEFT LEG 25 KICKS IN 1MINITE SINGLE LEG

III. PAD KICKING RIGHT LEG 25 KICKS IN 1MINITE SINGLE LEG

Note: I,II and III Rest for 1 ½ minutes of each kick, Do all kicks accordingly

Thursday: Same as on Tuesday Schedule

WEDNESDAY: SPEED TRAINING OF PUNCHES

4th & 5th week schedule

(i) Knuckle pushups, Close fist and keep knuckle on ground with shoulder width distance and go down and come up or palms pushups Do 12 pushups and 75 punches in 1 minute.

(ii) Single hand knuckle or palms pushups: Do one hand knuckle pushups 12 times one hand 40 punches in 1 minute and Change knuckles. Do alternate hands Do 2 sets

(iii) Power pushups for speed & power punches
Sit on kneeling position with palms facing ground and jump forward onto your palms on the Floor and Do 3 sets and get up and Do 150 punches in 3 minutes.

(iv) Pushing the kit bag and speed punch exercise: pushing the kit bag and 2 hands punches alternatively .Do 25 sets

SPEED UNDER WATER KICKS & UNDER WATER PUNCHES

Sunday 4th & 5th week schedule, water workout (water must be chest level)

I. Under water kicks Do 1 to 8 kicks each leg 10 kicks (total 20 kicks) in 1 minute
Do below mentioned kicks

1.Inner edge kick

2.Thrust kick

3.Side kick

4.Spinning kick

5.Round house kick

6. Hook kick

7. Outer edge kick

8. Hook kick and side kick with holding wall

II. a. Running in the water :
Running in the water 12 meters

b. Side Running in the water :
Running in the water right side 12 meters and left side 12 meters

c. knee raising in the water :
Knee raising in the water each leg 30 times (Total 60 times)

d. punches in the water :
(i) 75 double punches in the water with alternative hands
(ii)50 single hands punches with the left hand and right hand (Total 100 punches)

e. check every week the speed of every individual kicks in 1 minute and make a table of improvement (minimum kicks must be 140 kicks in 1 minute in Air every week)

SQUATS KICKS

Sunday Body Weight Squats Kicks below following kicks

4th & 5th week schedule

Sit on squat and get up and kick Down heel kick with one squat 2 kicks with the Right leg and left leg and sit. Do 10 kicks each leg (i.e. Total 20 kicks) in 1 minute.

Sit on squat and get up and kick inner edge with Right leg and left leg and sit. Do 10 kicks each leg (i.e. Total 20 kicks) in 1 minute.

Sit on squat and get up and kick outer edge with left leg and Right leg and sit. Do 10 kicks each leg (i.e. Total 20 kicks) in 1 minute.

Sit on squat and get up and kick front thrust kick with Right leg and with the Left leg and sit. Do 10 kicks each leg (i.e. Total 20 kicks) in 1 minute.

Sit on squat and get up and kick side kick with Right leg and with the Left leg and sit. Do 10 kicks each leg (i.e. Total 20 kicks) in 1 minute.

Sit on squat and get up and kick front side kick with Right leg and with the Left leg and sit. Do 10 kicks each leg (i.e. Total 20 kicks) in 1 minute.

Sit on squat and get up and kick Round house kick with Left leg and with the Right leg and sit. Do 10 kicks each leg (i.e. Total 20 kicks) in 1 minute.

Sit on squat and get up and kick back kick with Right leg and with the Left leg and sit. Do 10 kicks each leg (i.e. Total 20 kicks) in 1 minute.

Sit on squat and get up and kick Hook kick with Left leg and with the Right leg and sit. Do 10 kicks each leg (i.e. Total 20 kicks) in 1 minute.

6^Th^ Week

Speed Training schedule for 15 Years and above

Speed Training schedule for 13 – 15 Years

Speed Training schedule for below 13 years

"Doing practice is for better than saying I will practice"

- Grand Master M. Jayanth Reddy

SPEED TRAINING OF KICKS- 15 YEAR AND ABOVE

Monday –I 6th week schedule

1 ½ kgs ANKLE (LEG) WEIGHTS KICKS (Alternative Legs)

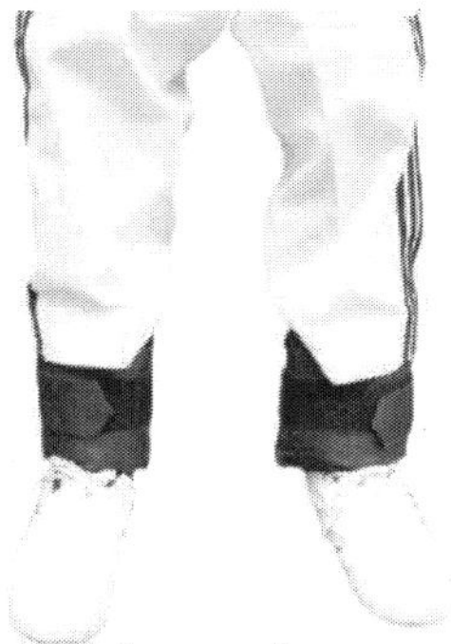

Wear an Ankle weight to your leg 11/2 kg each leg and start kicking all the kicks as shown in the pictures below. Each kick you need to do a minimum of 45 kicks each leg in 1 minute each Rest for 2 minute. Do all 1 to 10 kicks.

1.DOWN HEEL KICK, ALTERNATIVE LEGS

2.SIDE KICK, ALTERNATIVE LEGS

3.SPINNING CART WHEEL KICK, ALTERNATIVE LEGS

4.HOOK KICK, ALTERNATIVE LEGS

5.TRUST KICK ALTENATIVE LEG

6. INNER EDGE KICKS ALTERNATIVE LEGS

7. FRONT SIDE KICKS ALTERNATIVE LEGS

8. ROUND HOUSE KICK ALTERNATIVE LEGS

9. OUTER EDGE KICK ALTERNATIVE LEGS

10. BACK KICK AND DO ALTERNATIVE LEG

II. 1 ½ kgs of Ankle Weight kick Controlling:

Do only 4 Kicks i.e., (1) Thrust Kick (2) Side Kick (3) Round House Kick (4) Back Kick Control Each Leg at hips minimum do control for 20 to 30 seconds without any support. See Picture A,B,C and D, Do 2 sets each.

Pic-A

Thrust Kick, Alternative Legs

Pic-B

Side Kick, Alternative

Pic-C

Round House Kick Alternative

Pic-D

Back Kick do with Alternative Leg

III. Sitting kicks with 1 ½ kgs Ankle Weight:

Do only 4 kicks (1) snap kicks (2) Side kick (3) Round house kick (4) Hook kick.
Do each kick 125 times alternative legs Lie down on back and wear 1 ½ kgs Ankle weight and kick continuously snap kicks for 50 to 75 kicks see pic-P1 ,pic- P2 and p3.

Pic-P1

Pic-P2

Pic-P3

Kneel led down and sit and hands support on the ground and raise your Right leg Right side and kick side kick continuously 50 to 75 kicks with wearing 1 ½ kg Ankle weights and change the leg and do with other leg same. See pic-P4 and pic-P5.

Pic-P4

pic-P5

Kneel led down and sit and hands support on the ground and kick round house kick sideways 50 to 75 times each leg with wearing 1 ½ kgs Ankle weight. See pic-P6 and pic-P7

Pic- P6

Pic-P7

Kneel led down and sit and hands support on the ground and kick Hook kick sideways 50 to 75 times each leg wearing 1 ½ kgs Ankle weight. See pic-P8 and pic-P9.

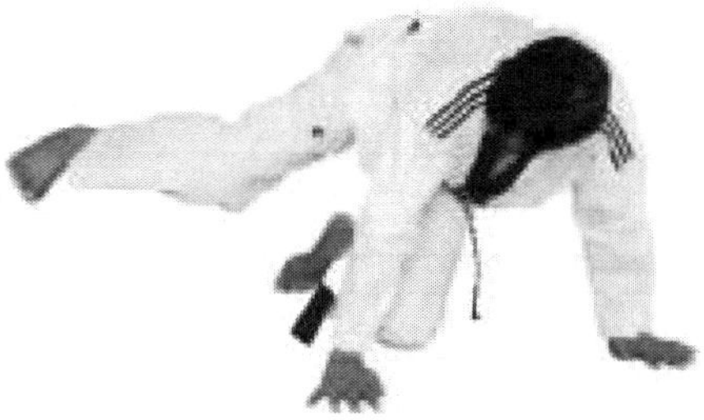

Pic-P8

Pic-P9

SPEED TRAINING OF PUNCHES - 15 YEAR AND ABOVE

Monday –I 6th week schedule

1kg HAND WEIGHTS (Alternative Hands)

(a) Horse stand Horse stand and hold 1 kg hand weight and Do 110 punches with alternative hands with 1kg hand weight in 1 minute See picture 1 and 2

Pic -1

Pic -2

(b) Stand in front forward stance and punch with single Right hand over the left open hand (Bend at elbow in the front) 60 punches with Single hand with 1kg hand weight in 1 minute

And change the hand i.e. change to left hand And punch with the same as Right hand punch.

See picture 3,4,5 and 6

Pic -3

Pic -4

Pic -5

Pic -6

(c) Speed sitting hand weights punches Sit on chair or stool and punch at least 90 times with alternative hand (with left hand and right hand)

Variation: your can do this sitting punches by blind folded i.e. with closing eyes, by imagining you are smashing with punch. See picture 7 and 8

Pic -7

Pic -8

(D) Biceps Forearm Triceps Strengthening Exercises for Speed:

Bicep Exercise 1

Hold 10 pounds in left hand and pull till chest. This will strengthen the biceps. Do with other hand each 3 sets of 20 times. Refer pictures A, B , A1 and B1

Pic -A Pic -B Pic -A1 Pic - B1

Bicep Exercise 2

Sit on chair and take 15 pounds hand dumbbell and pull up to chest level 20 repetitions each hand alternatively. Refer pictures A, B, C and D.

Pic -A Pic -B Pic -B Pic -D

Triceps Strengthening 3

Horse stance with barbell weight back of you and slightly bend forward your upper body and lift weight 15 pounds. See picture A.

Pic - A

Biceps Strengthening 4

Stand with barbell weight on your hand forward pull weight up to chest and withdraw to thighs. Do with 20 pounds increases according to your capacity. Do at least 20 repetitions Do 3 sets. . See picture A.

Pic -A

Forearm Exercise 5

Forearm and wrist strengthening

Stand with holding one sided dumbbell 8 pounds (approximately) sideways should be besides you and pull up as high as possible, Front side. Do with left hand and with right hand. This exercise will strengthen wrist, forearm. See pictures A, B, A1 and B1.

Pic - A

Pic - B

Pic – A1

Pic – B1

Forearm Strengthening Exercise 6

Stand with holding one sided dumbbell 8 pounds (approximately) with right hand beside your thigh and pull up and down back side 20 times each hand alternately. See picture C and D.

Pic - C

Pic - D

Wrist Strengthening Exercises7

Sit on chair and hold one side dumbbell 8 pounds (approximately) with Right forearm on the thighs and twist to left and right side with maximum strain. Do with other hand, Do 15 times each. See pictures A, B, C, D, E, and F

Pic -A

Pic - B

Pic - C

Pic -D

Pic - E

Pic - F

Triceps Exercise 8

Sit on chair and hold one side Drum bell 8 to 10 pounds (approximately) with Right hand Back side and pull up and Down, See pictures S1, S2, S3, and S4

Pic – S1

Pic – S2

Pic – S3

Pic – S4

Forearm Strengthening 9

Sit on stool and holding bar with 15 pounds (approximately) weight with palm facing sky, as shown in picture with hands 10" inches apart and pull up your wrist to you and pull down 20 times. Note: Keep forearm and elbow on the thighs to balance the weight. See pictures A and B.

Pic – A Pic - B

Forearm strengthening 10

Sit on stool and holding bar15 pounds (approximately) as shown in picture with hands 10" inches apart and pull to you and pull down 20 times. Note: Keep forearm and elbow on the thighs to balance the weight with palm facing floor in punching position. See pictures C and D.

Pic – C Pic – D

Forearm Strengthening Exercises 11

Holding 12" to 15" long rod 8 pounds (approximately) tightly on the right side and twist 180degrees for 30 times and change the hand and continue. See pictures A, B, C

Variations: You can hold 2 rods either side of each hand and twist them.

Pic - A

Pic - B

Pic - C

Forearm Strengthening 12

Hold 12" to 14" rod 8 pounds (approximately) in front of you and twist left and right 180 degrees angle with left hand 20 to 30 repetitions and change to right hand and do the same repetitions. See pictures A, B, C, D, E and F.

Pic - A Pic – B Pic – C Pic- D Pic – E Pic - F

Triceps Strengthening Exercise 13

Keep index and thumb of each hand join together and go for pushups with leg stretch out without bending knees. Do this exercise for 10 to 20 times daily. See pictures A and B.

.

Pic A

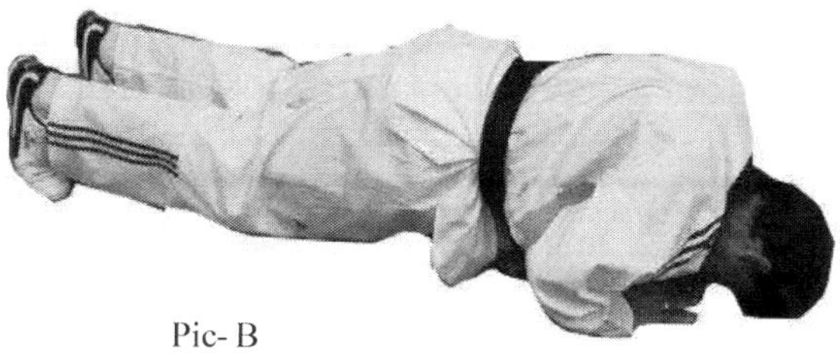

Pic- B

Friday: Same as on Monday Schedule

SPEED PEDDLE KICKS(kicking on pad)

Tuesday 6th week schedule

I. PAD KICKING EACH LEG 35 KICKS 1 TO 15 KICKS

(1) Push kick

(2) Front thrust kick

(3) Side kick

(4) Round house kick

(5) Back kick

(6) Outer edge kick

(7) Inner edge kick

(8) Down heel kick

(9) Hook kick

(10) Jumping side kick

(11) Jumping Round house kick

(12) Jumping Back kick

(13) Spin kick

(14) Jumping spin kick

(15) Scissor kick

Jumping thrust kick

Push Kick on Pad -1

Front thrust kick on pad -2

Side kick on pad -3

Round house on pad-4

Back kick on pad – 5

Outer edge kick on pad – 6

Inner edge kick on pad -7

Down heel kick on pad -8

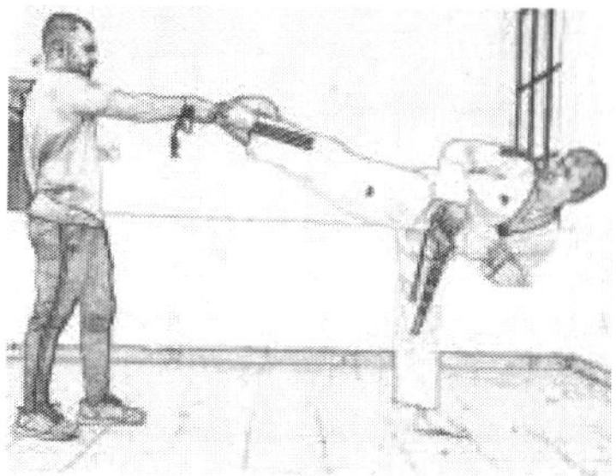

Hook kick on pad – 9

Jumping side kick on pad – 10

Jumping Round house kick on pad - 11

Jumping Back kick on pad – 12

Jumping spin kick on pad - 13

Front Side kick -14

Scissor kick-15

II. PAD KICKING LEFT LEG 35 KICKS IN 30 SECONDS SINGLE LEG

III. PAD KICKING RIGHT LEG 35 KICKS IN 30 SECONDS SINGLE LEG

Note: I,II and III Rest for 1 ½ minutes of each kick, Do all kicks accordingly

Thursday: Same as on Tuesday Schedule

SPEED NYLON / TUBE KICKING

Wednesday 6th week schedule

Speed Kicking With Tube

Tie bicycle tube or nylon thread and tie to your ankle and kick all kicks 35 times in 45 seconds alternative leg. Rest for 1 minute with each kick.
Do all kicks below mentioned stationary kicks 35 kicks in 40 seconds and 20 jumping kicks in 50 seconds.

Speed Kicking With Tube

Tie bicycle tube or nylon thread and tie to your ankle and kick all kicks 35 times with each leg. This improves kicking speed. Once in a week you can do single leg kick and alternative leg kicks.

Side Kick with Left

Side Kick with Right

Hook

Outer edge kick

Round house kick

Thrust kick

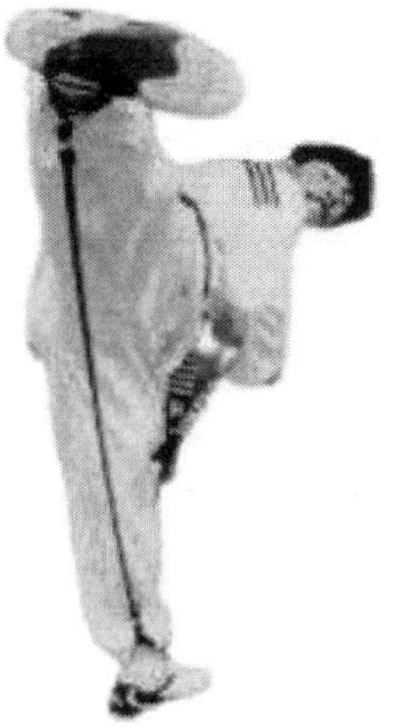

Back kick

Back kick

Jumping Round house kick

Jumping side kick with Right leg

Jumping side kick with Left leg

SPEED KICKING ON PAD WITH TIEING TUBE

Down heel kick with tube

Inner edge kick with tube

Outer edge kick with tube

Front thrust kick with tube

Round house kick with tube

Side kick with tube

Back kick with tube

Hook kick with tube

Jumping Round house kick with tube

Jumping Back kick with tube

Jumping side kick with tube

Jumping thrust kick with tube

Turning Jumping Round house
kick with tube Pic -A1

Turning Jumping Round house
kick with tube pic-A2

Turning Jumping Round house kick
with tube Pic -A3

WEDNESDAY: <u>SPEED TRAINING OF PUNCHES</u>

6th week schedule

(vi) Knuckle pushups, Close fist and keep knuckle on ground with shoulder width distance and go down and come up. Do 30 pushups and 150 punches in 1 minute. See pictures A and B and C

Pic - A

Pic- C

Pic - B

(ii) Single hand knuckle pushups: Do one hand knuckle pushups 15 times one hand 40 punches in 1 minute and Change knuckles. Do alternate hands Do 2 sets. See picture A

Pic - A

(iii) Power pushups for speed & power punches
Sit on kneeling position with palms facing ground and jump forward onto your palms on the floor as shown in pictures A and B. Do 5 sets and get up and Do 200 punches in 3 minutes.

Pic A

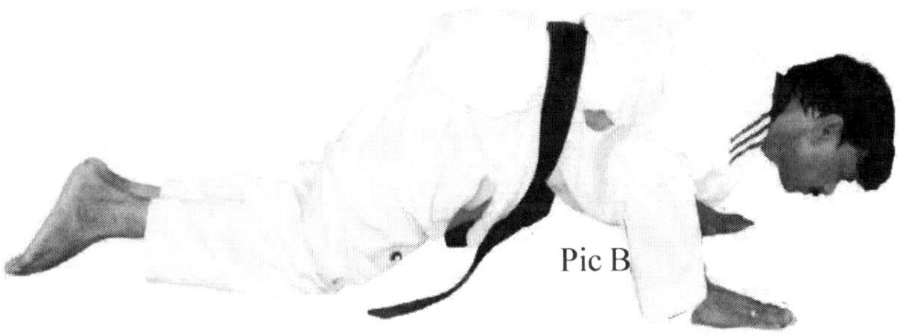

Pic B

(iv) Pushing the kit bag and speed punch exercise: pushing the kit bag and 2 hands punches alternatively .Do 40 sets See pic- P1, P2 and P3

Pic –P1

Pic –P2

Pic –P3

Saturday: Tube kicking with single leg

6th week schedule

Tube kicking with single leg 40 kicks in 45 seconds one minute Rest between each single leg kicks Do all kicks 40 times in 45 seconds each leg. Below mentioned kicks.

Side Kick with Left

Side Kick with Right

Hook

Outer edge kick

Round house kick

Thrust kick

Back kick

Back kick

Jumping Round house kick

SPEED UNDER WATER KICKS & UNDER WATER PUNCHES

Sunday 6th week schedule, water workout (water must be chest level)

I. Under water kicks Do 1 to 8 kicks each leg 15 kicks (total 30 kicks) in 1 minute

1.Inner edge kick

2.Thrust kick

3.Side kick

4.Spinning kick

5.Round house kick

6. Hook kick

7. Outer edge kick

8. Hook kick and side kick with holding wall

II. a. Running in the water :
Running in the water 25 meters

b. Side Running in the water :
Running in the water right side 25 meters and left side 25 meters

c. knee raising in the water :
Knee raising in the water each leg 50 times (Total 100 times)

d. punches in the water :
(i)150 double punches in the water with alternative hands
(ii)100 single hands punches with the left hand and right hand (Total 200 punches)

e. check the speed of every individual kicks in 1 minute and make a of table improvement (minimum kicks must be 160 kicks in 1 minute)

f. check the speed of every individual kicks in 1 minute and make a of table improvement

SQUATS KICKS

Sunday Body Weight Squats Kicks below following kicks

6th week schedule

Sit on squat and get up and kick Down heel kick with one squat 2 kicks the Right leg and left leg and sit. Do 15 kicks each leg (i.e. Total 30 kicks) See pic-L1,pic-L2,pic-L3 and pic-4

Pic-L1

Pic-L2

Pic-L3

Pic-L4

Sit on squat and get up and kick inner edge with Right leg and left leg and sit. Do 15 kicks each leg (i.e. Total 30 kicks) see pic- L5 and pic-L6.

Sit on squat and get up and kick outer edge with left leg and Right leg and sit. Do 15 kicks each leg (i.e. Total 30 kicks) See pic- L7 and pic-L8.

Sit on squat and get up and kick front thrust kick with Right leg and with the Left leg and sit. Do 15 kicks each leg (i.e. Total 30 kicks) See pic-L9 and pic-L10

Pic-L5

Pic-L6

Pic-L7

Pic-L8

Pic-L9

Pic-L10

Sit on squat and get up and kick side kick with Right leg and with the Left leg and sit. Do 15 kicks each leg (i.e. Total 30 kicks) See pic-L11 and pic-L12.

Sit on squat and get up and kick front side kick with Right leg and with the Left leg and sit. Do 15 kicks each leg (i.e. Total 30 kicks) See pic-L13 and pic-L14.

Sit on squat and get up and kick Round house kick with Left leg and with the Right leg and sit. Do 15 kicks each leg (i.e. Total 30 kicks) See pic-L15 and pic-L16.

Pic-L11

Pic-L12

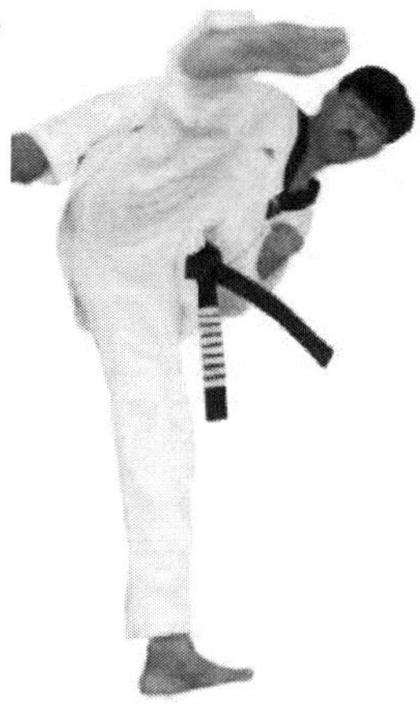

Pic-L13

Pic-L14

Pic-L15

Pic-L16 (side view)

Sit on squat and get up and kick Back kick with Right leg and with the Left leg and sit. Do 15 kicks each leg (i.e. Total 30 kicks) See pic-L17,pic-L18 and L19 Back kick in Front View.

Pic-L17

Pic-L18

Back kick Front view Pic-L19

Sit on squat and get up and kick Hook kick with Left leg and with the Right leg and sit. Do 15 kicks each leg (i.e. Total 30 kicks) See pic-L20,pic-L21 Front view.

Pic-L20 (Side View)

Hook kick front viewPic-L21

SPEED TRAINING OF KICKS-13 TO 15 YEARS

Monday –I 6th week schedule

1kg ANKLE (LEG) WEIGHTS KICKS(Alternative Legs)

Wear a Ankle weight to your leg 1 kg each leg and start kicking all the kicks as shown in the pictures below. Each kick you need to do a minimum of 50 kicks each leg in 1 minute Rest for 2 minute. Do all 1 to 10 kicks.

1. down heel kick, alternative legs
2. Side Kick, alternative Legs
3. Spinning cart wheel kick, alternative legs
4. Hook Kick, alternative Legs
5. Trust Kick alternative Leg
6. Inner edge kicks alternative legs
7. Front side kicks alternative legs
8. Round House Kick Alternative Legs
9. Outer Edge Kick Alternative Legs
10. Back Kick and Do Alternative Leg

II. 1kgs of Ankle Weight kick Controlling:

Do only 4 Kicks i.e., (1) Thrust Kick (2) Side Kick (3) Round House Kick (4) Back Kick

Control Each Leg at hips minimum do control for 30 seconds without any support.

III. Sitting kicks with 1 kg Ankle Weight:

Do only 4 kicks (1) snap kicks (2) Side kick (3) Round house kick (4) Hook kick.
Do each kick 80 times alternative legs Lie down on back and wear 1kgs Ankle weight and kick continuously snap kicks for 80 kicks

Kneel Led down and sit and hands support on the ground and raise your Right leg Right side and kick side kick continuously 40 kicks with wearing 1kg Ankle weights and change the leg and do with other leg same.

Kneel down and sit and hands support on the ground and kick round house kick sideways 40 times each leg with wearing 1kgs Ankle weight.

Kneel down and sit and hands support on the ground and kick Hook kick sideways 40 times each leg wearing 1kg Ankle weight

SPEED TRAINING OF PUNCHES - 13 TO 15 YEARS

Monday –I 6th week schedule

½ kg HAND WEIGHTS (Alternative Hands)

(a) Horse stand and hold ½ kg hand weight and Do 70 punches with alternative hands in 1 minute

(b) Stand in front forward stance and punch with single Right hand over the left open hand (Bend at elbow in the front) 30 punches with Single hand with ½ kg hand weight in 1 minute

And change the hand i.e. change to left hand and punch with the same as Right hand punch.

(C) Speed sitting hand weights punches Sit on chair or stool and punch at least 50 times with alternative hand (with left hand and right hand)

Variation: your can do this sitting punches by blind folded i.e. with closing eyes, by imagining you are smashing with punch.

(d) Forearm Exercise

Forearm and wrist strengthening

Stand with holding one sided dumbbell 8 pounds (approximately) sideways should be besides you and pull up as high as possible, Front side. Do with left hand and with right hand. This exercise will strengthen wrist, forearm.

(e) Forearm Strengthening Exercise

Stand with holding one sided dumbbell 8 pounds (approximately) with right hand beside your thigh and pull up and down back side 15 times each hand alternately.

(f) Wrist Strengthening Exercises

Sit on chair and hold one side dumbbell 8 pounds (approximately) with Right forearm on the thighs and twist to left and right side with maximum strain. Do with other hand, Do 12 times each.

g) Forearm Strengthening

Sit on stool and holding bar with 15 pounds (approximately) weight with palm facing sky, as shown in picture with hands 10" inches apart and pull up your wrist to you and pull down 16 times. Note: Keep forearm and elbow on the thighs to balance the weight

(h) Forearm strengthening

Sit on stool and holding bar15 pounds (approximately) as shown in picture with hands 10" inches apart and pull to you and pull down 12 times. Note: Keep forearm and elbow on the thighs to balance the weight with palm facing floor in punching position

(i)Forearm Strengthening Exercises

Holding 12" to 15" long rod 8 pounds (approximately) tightly on the right side and twist 180degrees for 22 times and change the hand and continue.

Variations: You can hold 2 rods either side of each hand and twist them.

(j)Forearm Strengthening

Hold 12" to 14" rod 8 pounds (approximately) in front of you and twist left and right 180 degrees angle with left hand 20 repetitions and change to right hand and do the same repetitions.

(k) Triceps Strengthening Exercise

Keep index and thumb of each hand join together and go for pushups with leg stretch out without bending knees. Do this exercise for 10 to 12 times daily.

Friday: Same as on Monday Schedule

SPEED PEDDLE KICKS(kicking on pad)

Tuesday 6th week schedule

I. PAD KICKING EACH LEG 30 KICKS 1 TO 15 KICKS

(1) Push kick

(2) Front thrust kick

(3) Side kick

(4) Round house kick

(5) Back kick

(6) Outer edge kick

(7) Inner edge kick

(8) Down heel kick

(9) Hook kick

(10) Jumping side kick

(11) Jumping Round house kick

(12) Jumping Back kick

(13) Spin kick

(14) Jumping spin kick

(15) Scissor kick

II. PAD KICKING LEFT LEG 30 KICKS IN 30 SECONDS SINGLE LEG

III. PAD KICKING RIGHT LEG 30 KICKS IN 30 SECONDS SINGLE LEG

Note: I,II and III Rest for 1 ½ minutes of each kick, Do all kicks accordingly

Thursday: Same as on Tuesday Schedule

SPEED NYLON / TUBE KICKING

Wednesday 6th week schedule

Speed Kicking With Tube

Tie bicycle tube or nylon thread and tie to your ankle and kick all kicks 30 times in 45 seconds alternative leg. Rest for 1 minute with each kick in air or kicking pad.
Do all kicks below mentioned stationary kicks 32 kicks in 45 seconds and 16 jumping kicks in 50 seconds.

Speed Kicking With Tube

Tie bicycle tube or nylon thread and tie to your ankle and kick all kicks 32 times with each leg. This improves kicking speed. Once in a week you can do single leg kick and alternative leg kicks. Do below mentioned kicks.

1. Side Kick with Left and Right Leg
2. Outer edge kick with Left and Right Leg
3. Inner edge kick with Left and Right Leg
4. Thrust kick with Left and Right Leg
5. Back kick with Left and Right Leg
6. Round house kick with Left and Right Leg
7. Hook Kick with Left and Right Leg
8. Jumping Round house kick with Left and Right Leg
9. Jumping side kick with Left and Right Leg
10. Down heel kick with Left and Right Leg
11. Jumping Thrust kick with Left and Right Leg
12. Jumping Back kick with Left and Right Leg

WEDNESDAY: <u>SPEED TRAINING OF PUNCHES</u>

6th week schedule

(i) Knuckle pushups, Close fist and keep knuckle on ground with shoulder width distance and go down and come up. Do 22 push ups and 80 punches in 1 minute.

(ii) Single hand knuckle pushups: Do one hand knuckle pushups 12 times one hand 22 punches in 1 minute and Change knuckles. Do alternate hands Do 2 sets

(iii) Power pushups for speed & power punches
Sit on kneeling position with palms facing ground and jump forward onto your palms on the Floor and Do 4 sets and get up and Do 170 punches in 2 minutes.

(iv) Pushing the kit bag and speed punch exercise: pushing the kit bag and 2 hands punches alternatively .Do 32 sets

Saturday: Tube kicking with single leg

6th week schedule

Tube kicking with single leg 32 kicks in 45 seconds one minute or 2 minutes Rest between each single leg kicks

Do all kicks 32 times in 45 seconds each leg. Below mentioned kicks.

1. Side Kick with Left and Right Leg
2. Hook Kick with Left and Right Leg
3. Outer edge kick with Left and Right Leg
4. Round house kick with Left and Right Leg
5. *Thrust kick* with Left and Right Leg
6. Back kick with Left and Right Leg
7. Jumping Round house kick with Left and Right Leg
8. Inner edge kick with Left and Right Leg

SPEED UNDER WATER KICKS & UNDER WATER PUNCHES

Sunday 6th week schedule, water workout (water must be chest level)

I. Under water kicks Do 1 to 8 kicks each leg 13 kicks (total 26 kicks) in 1 minute
Do below mentioned kicks

1.Inner edge kick

2.Thrust kick

3.Side kick

4.Spinning kick

5.Round house kick

6. Hook kick

7. Outer edge kick

8. Hook kick and side kick with holding wall

II. a. Running in the water :
Running in the water 25 meters

b. Side Running in the water :
Running in the water right side 25 meters and left side 25 meters

c. knee raising in the water :
Knee raising in the water each leg 50 times (Total 100 times)

d. punches in the water :
(i)125 double punches in the water with alternative hands
(ii)80 single hands punches with the left hand and right hand (Total 160 punches)

e. check the speed of every individual kicks in 1 minute and make a table of improvement (minimum kicks must be 180 kicks in 1 minute in Air every week)

SQUATS KICKS

Sunday Body Weight Squats Kicks below following kicks 6th week schedule

Sit on squat and get up and kick Down heel kick with one squat 2 kicks with the Right leg and left leg and sit. Do 15 kicks each leg (i.e. Total 30 kicks)

Sit on squat and get up and kick inner edge with Right leg and left leg and sit. Do 15 kicks each leg (i.e. Total 30kicks.

Sit on squat and get up and kick outer edge with left leg and Right leg and sit. Do 15 kicks each leg (i.e. Total 30 kicks).

Sit on squat and get up and kick front thrust kick with Right leg and with the Left leg and sit. Do 15 kicks each leg (i.e. Total 30 kicks) .

Sit on squat and get up and kick side kick with Right leg and with the Left leg and sit. Do 15 kicks each leg (i.e. Total 30 kicks).

Sit on squat and get up and kick front side kick with Right leg and with the Left leg and sit. Do 15 kicks each leg (i.e. Total 30 kicks).

Sit on squat and get up and kick Round house kick with Left leg and with the Right leg and sit. Do 15 kicks each leg (i.e. Total 30 kicks).

Sit on squat and get up and kick Back kick with Right leg and with the Left leg and sit. Do 15 kicks each leg (i.e. Total 30 kicks).

Sit on squat and get up and kick Hook kick with Left leg and with the Right leg and sit. Do 15 kicks each leg (i.e. Total 30 kicks).

SPEED TRAINING OF KICKS - BELOW 13 YEARS

Monday –I 6th & 7th week schedule

110 KICKS IN 2 MINITUES

Each kick you need to do a minimum of 55 kicks each leg in 1 minute Rest for 2 minute. Do all 1 to 10 kicks. Below mention kicks

1. down heel kick, alternative legs
2. Side Kick, alternative Legs
3. Spinning cart wheel kick, alternative legs
4. Hook Kick, alternative Legs
5. Trust Kick alternative Leg
6. Inner edge kicks alternative legs
7. Front side kicks alternative legs
8. Round House Kick Alternative Legs
9. Outer Edge Kick Alternative Legs
10. Back Kick and Do Alternative Leg

II. kick Controlling:

Do only 4 Kicks i.e., (1) Thrust Kick (2) Side Kick (3) Round House Kick (4) Back Kick

Control Each Leg at hips minimum do control for 30 to 35 seconds without any support.

III. Sitting kicks :

Do only 4 kicks (1) snap kicks (2) Side kick (3) Round house kick (4) Hook kick.
Do each kick 90 times alternative legs Lie down on back and kick continuously snap kicks start from 45 kicks to 90 kicks

Kneel Led down and sit and hands support on the ground and raise your Right leg Right side and kick side kick continuously 45 to 90 and change the leg and do with other leg same.

Kneel down and sit and hands support on the ground and kick round house kick sideways 45 to 90 times each leg.

Kneel down and sit and hands support on the ground and kick Hook kick sideways 45 to 90 times each leg.

Variation : kicks on x-ray film. You can do all kicks and all punches on x-ray film each kick 18 times and 90 punch with 2 hands.

SPEED TRAINING OF PUNCHES - BELOW 13 YEARS

Monday –I 6th & 7th week schedule

160 punches in 1 minute (Alternative Hands)

(a) Horse stand and Do 160 punches with alternative hands in 1 minute Do 2 sets.

(b) Stand in front forward stance and punch with single Right hand over the left open hand (Bend at elbow in the front) 90 punches with Single hand with in 1 minute Do 2 sets And change the hand i.e. change to left hand and punch with the same as Right hand punch.

(c) Speed sitting hand punches Sit on chair or stool and punch at least 125 times with alternative hand (with left hand and right hand) Do 2 sets.
Variation: your can do this sitting punches by blind folded i.e. with closing eyes, by imagining you are smashing with punch.

(d) Punches on x-ray film: you can practices 90 with each hand (total 180 punches)

(e) Triceps Strengthening Exercise
Keep index and thumb of each hand join together and go for pushups with leg stretch out without bending knees. Do this exercise for 10 to 15 times daily.

Friday: Same as on Monday Schedule

SPEED PEDDLE KICKS(kicking on pad)

Tuesday 6th &7th week schedule

I. PAD KICKING EACH LEG 35 KICKS 1 TO 15 KICKS

(1) Push kick - 35 kicks each leg
(2) Front thrust kick " "
(3) Side kick " "
(4) Round house kick " "
(5) Back kick " "
(6) Outer edge kick " "
(7) Inner edge kick " "
(8) Down heel kick " "
(9) Hook kick " "
(10) Jumping side kick " "
(11) Jumping Round house kick " "

(12) Jumping Back kick - 25 kicks each leg

(13) Spin kick -35 kicks each leg

(14) Jumping spin kick -25 kicks each leg

(15) Scissor kick - 35 kicks each leg

II. PAD KICKING LEFT LEG 35 KICKS IN 1MINITE SINGLE LEG

III. PAD KICKING RIGHT LEG 35 KICKS IN 1MINITE SINGLE LEG

Note: I,II and III Rest for 1 ½ minutes of each kick, Do all kicks accordingly

Thursday: Same as on Tuesday Schedule

WEDNESDAY: SPEED TRAINING OF PUNCHES

6th & 7th week schedule

(i) Knuckle pushups, Close fist and keep knuckle on ground with shoulder width distance and go down and come up or palms pushups Do 15 pushups and 90 punches in 1 minute.

(ii) Single hand knuckle or palms pushups: Do one hand knuckle pushups 15 times one hand 50 punches in 1 minute and Change knuckles. Do alternate hands Do 2 sets

(iii) Power pushups for speed & power punches
Sit on kneeling position with palms facing ground and jump forward onto your palms on the Floor and Do 3 sets and get up and Do 180 punches in 3 minutes.

(iv) Pushing the kit bag and speed punch exercise: pushing the kit bag and 2 hands punches alternatively .Do 35 sets

SPEED UNDER WATER KICKS & UNDER WATER PUNCHES

Sunday 6th & 7th week schedule, water workout (water must be chest level)

I. Under water kicks Do 1 to 8 kicks each leg 12 kicks (total 24 kicks) in 1 minute
Do below mentioned kicks

1.Inner edge kick

2.Thrust kick

3.Side kick

4.Spinning kick

5.Round house kick

6. Hook kick

7. Outer edge kick

8. Hook kick and side kick with holding wall

II. a. Running in the water :
Running in the water 15 meters

b. Side Running in the water :
Running in the water right side 15 meters and left side 15 meters

c. knee raising in the water :
Knee raising in the water each leg 35 times (Total 70 times)

d. punches in the water :
(i) 90 double punches in the water with alternative hands
(ii)65 single hands punches with the left hand and right hand (Total 130 punches)

e. check every week the speed of every individual kicks in 1 minute and make a table of improvement (minimum kicks must be 160 kicks in 1 minute in Air every week)

SQUATS KICKS

Sunday Body Weight Squats Kicks below following kicks

6th & 7th week schedule

Sit on squat and get up and kick Down heel kick with one squat 2 kicks with the Right leg and left leg and sit. Do 12 kicks each leg (i.e. Total 24 kicks) in 1 minute.

Sit on squat and get up and kick inner edge with Right leg and left leg and sit. Do 12 kicks each leg (i.e. Total 24 kicks) in 1 minute.

Sit on squat and get up and kick outer edge with left leg and Right leg and sit. Do 12 kicks each leg (i.e. Total 24 kicks) in 1 minute.

Sit on squat and get up and kick front thrust kick with Right leg and with the Left leg and sit. Do 12 kicks each leg (i.e. Total 24 kicks) in 1 minute.

Sit on squat and get up and kick side kick with Right leg and with the Left leg and sit. Do 12 kicks each leg (i.e. Total 24 kicks) in 1 minute.

Sit on squat and get up and kick front side kick with Right leg and with the Left leg and sit. Do 12 kicks each leg (i.e. Total 24 kicks) in 1 minute.

Sit on squat and get up and kick Round house kick with Left leg and with the Right leg and sit. Do 12 kicks each leg (i.e. Total 24 kicks) in 1 minute.

Sit on squat and get up and kick Back kick with Right leg and with the Left leg and sit. Do 12 kicks each leg (i.e. Total 24 kicks) in 1 minute.

Sit on squat and get up and kick Hook kick with Left leg and with the Right leg and sit. Do 12 kicks each leg (i.e. Total 24 kicks) in 1 minute.

7^Th^ Week

7

Th

Week

Speed Training schedule for 15 Years and above

Speed Training schedule for 13 – 15 Years

Speed Training schedule for below 13 years

"The speed of my kick is not the supreme but how I made that kick"

\-

\- Grand Master M. Jayanth Reddy

SPEED TRAINING OF KICKS- 15 YEAR AND ABOVE

Monday –I 7th week schedule

2kgs ANKLE (LEG) WEIGHTS KICKS (Alternative Legs)

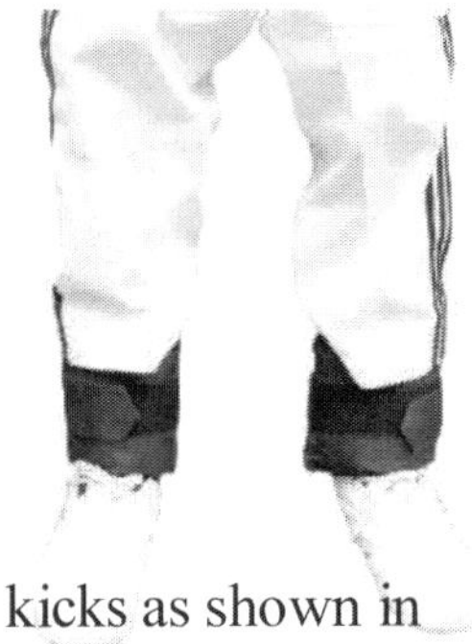

Wear an Ankle weight to your leg 2 kg each leg and start kicking all the kicks as shown in the pictures below. Each kick you need to do a minimum of 50 kicks each leg in 1 minute each Rest for 2 minute. Do all 1 to 10 kicks.

1.DOWN HEEL KICK, ALTERNATIVE LEGS

2.SIDE KICK, ALTERNATIVE LEGS

3.SPINNING CART WHEEL KICK, ALTERNATIVE LEGS

4.HOOK KICK, ALTERNATIVE LEGS

5.TRUST KICK ALTENATIVE LEG

6. INNER EDGE KICKS ALTERNATIVE LEGS

7. FRONT SIDE KICKS ALTERNATIVE LEGS

8. ROUND HOUSE KICK ALTERNATIVE LEGS

9. OUTER EDGE KICK ALTERNATIVE LEGS

10. BACK KICK AND DO ALTERNATIVE LEG

II. 2kgs of Ankle Weight kick Controlling:

Do only 4 Kicks i.e., (1) Thrust Kick (2) Side Kick (3) Round House Kick (4) Back Kick Control Each Leg at hips minimum do control for 20 to 30 seconds without any support. See Picture A,B,C and D, Do 2 sets each.

Pic-A

Thrust Kick, Alternative Legs

Pic-B

Side Kick, Alternative

Pic-C

Round House Kick Alternative

Pic-D

Back Kick do with Alternative Leg

III. Sitting kicks with 2 kgs Ankle weight:

Do only 4 kicks (1) snap kicks (2) Side kick (3) Round house kick (4) Hook kick.
Do each kick 120 times alternative legs Lie down on back and wear 2 kgs Ankle weight and kick continuously snap kicks for 50 to 75 kicks see pic-P1 ,pic- P2 and p3.

Pic-P1

Pic-P2

Pic-P3

Kneel led down and sit and hands support on the ground and raise your Right leg Right side and kick side kick continuously 50 to 75 kicks with wearing 2kg Ankle weights and change the leg and do with other leg same. See pic-P4 and pic-P5.

pic-P4

pic-P5

Kneel led down and sit and hands support on the ground and kick round house kick sideways 50 to 75 times each leg with wearing 2kgs Ankle weight. See pic-P6 and pic-P7

pic-P6

pic-P7

Kneel led down and sit and hands support on the ground and kick Hook kick sideways 50 to 75 times each leg wearing 2kgs Ankle weight. See pic-P8 and pic-P9.

pic-P8

pic-P9

SPEED TRAINING OF PUNCHES - 15 YEAR AND ABOVE

Monday –I 7th week schedule

1kgs HAND WEIGHTS (Alternative Hands)

(a) Horse stand Horse stand and hold 1 kg hand weight and Do 110 punches with alternative hands with 1kg hand weight in 1 minute See picture 1 and 2

Pic -1

Pic -2

(b) Stand in front forward stance and punch with single Right hand over the left open hand (Bend at elbow in the front) 60 punches with Single hand with 1kg hand weight in 1 minute

And change the hand i.e. change to left hand and punch with the same as Right hand punch. See picture 3,4,5 and 6

Pic -3

Pic -4

Pic -5

Pic -6

(c) Speed sitting hand weights punches Sit on chair or stool and punch at least 90 times with alternative hand (with left hand and right hand)

Variation: your can do this sitting punches by blind folded i.e. with closing eyes, by imagining you are smashing with punch. See picture 7 and 8

Pic -7

Pic -8

(D) Biceps Forearm Triceps Strengthening Exercises for Speed

Bicep Exercise 1

Hold 10 pounds in left hand and pull till chest. This will strengthen the biceps. Do with other hand each 3 sets of 20 times. Refer pictures A, B , A1 and B1

Pic -A

Pic -B

Pic -A1

Pic - B1

Bicep Exercise 2

Sit on chair and take 15 pounds hand dumbbell and pull up to chest level 20 repetitions each hand alternatively. Refer pictures A, B, C and D.

Pic -A

Pic -B

Pic -B

Pic -D

Triceps Strengthening 3

Horse stance with barbell weight back of you and slightly bend forward your upper body and lift weight 15 pounds. See picture A.

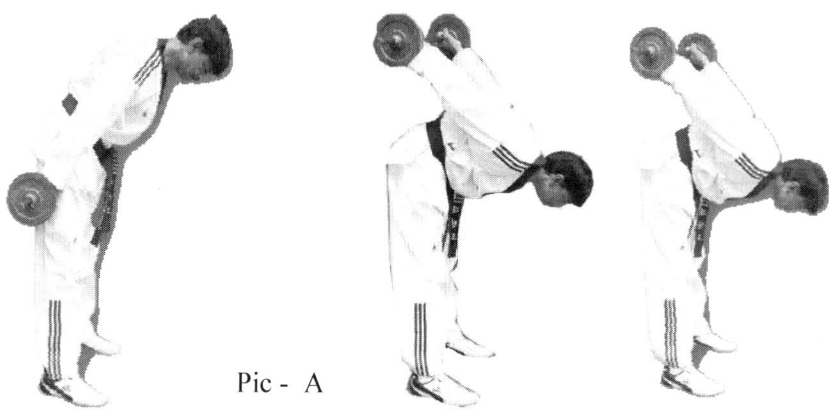
Pic - A

Biceps Strengthening 4

Stand with barbell weight on your hand forward pull weight up to chest and withdraw to thighs. Do with 20 pounds increases according to your capacity. Do at least 20 repetitions Do 3 sets. . See picture A.

Pic -A

Forearm Exercise 5

Forearm and wrist strengthening

Stand with holding one sided dumbbell 8 pounds (approximately) sideways should be besides you and pull up as high as possible, Front side. Do with left hand and with right hand. This exercise will strengthen wrist, forearm. See pictures A, B, A1 and B1.

Pic - A

Pic - B

Pic – A1

Pic – B1

Forearm Strengthening Exercise 6

Stand with holding one sided dumbbell 8 pounds (approximately) with right hand beside your thigh and pull up and down back side 20 times each hand alternately. See picture C and D.

Pic - C

Pic - D

Wrist Strengthening Exercises7

Sit on chair and hold one side dumbbell 8 pounds (approximately) with Right forearm on the thighs and twist to left and right side with maximum strain. Do with other hand, Do 15 times each. See pictures A, B, C, D, E, and F

Pic -A

Pic - B

Pic - C

Pic -D

Pic - E

Pic - F

Triceps Exercise 8

Sit on chair and hold one side Dumbbell 8 to 10 pounds (approximately) with Right hand Back side and pull up and Down, See pictures S1, S2, S3, and S4

Pic – S1

Pic – S2

Pic – S3

Pic – S4

Forearm Strengthening 9

Sit on stool and holding bar with 15 pounds (approximately) weight with palm facing sky, as shown in picture with hands 10" inches apart and pull up your wrist to you and pull down 20 times. Note: Keep forearm and elbow on the thighs to balance the weight. See pictures A and B.

Pic – A

Pic - B

Forearm strengthening 10

Sit on stool and holding bar15 pounds (approximately) as shown in picture with hands 10" inches apart and pull to you and pull down 20 times. Note: Keep forearm and elbow on the thighs to balance the weight with palm facing floor in punching position. See pictures C and D.

Pic – C

Pic – D

Forearm Strengthening Exercises 11

Holding 12" to 15" long rod 8 pounds (approximately) tightly on the right side and twist 180degrees for 30 times and change the hand and continue. See pictures A, B and C

Variations: You can hold 2 rods either side of each hand and twist them.

Pic - A

Pic - B

Pic - C

Forearm Strengthening 12

Hold 12" to 14" rod 8 pounds (approximately) in front of you and twist left and right 180 degrees angle with left hand 20 to 30 repetitions and change to right hand and do the same repetitions. See pictures A, B, C, D, E and F.

Pic - A

Pic – B

Pic – C

Pic- D

Pic – E

Pic - F

Triceps Strengthening Exercise 13

Keep index and thumb of each hand join together and go for pushups with leg stretch out without bending knees. Do this exercise for 10 to 20 times daily. See pictures A and B.

Pic A

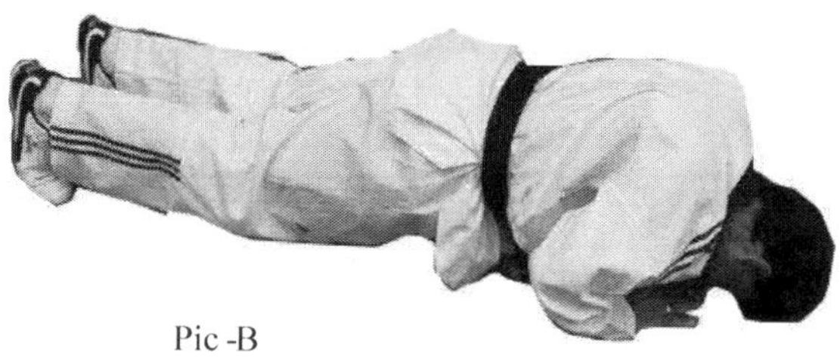

Pic -B

Friday: Same as on Monday Schedule

SPEED PEDDLE KICKS(kicking on pad)

Tuesday 7th week schedule

I. PAD KICKING EACH LEG 40 KICKS 1 TO 15 KICKS

(1) Push kick
(2) Front thrust kick
(3) Side kick
(4) Round house kick
(5) Back kick
(6) Outer edge kick
(7) Inner edge kick
(8) Down heel kick
(9) Hook kick
(10) Jumping side kick
(11) Jumping Round house kick
(12) Jumping Back kick
(13) Spin kick
(14) Jumping spin kick
(15) Scissor kick

Jumping thrust kick

Push Kick on Pad -1

Front thrust kick on pad -2

Side kick on pad -3

Round house on pad-4

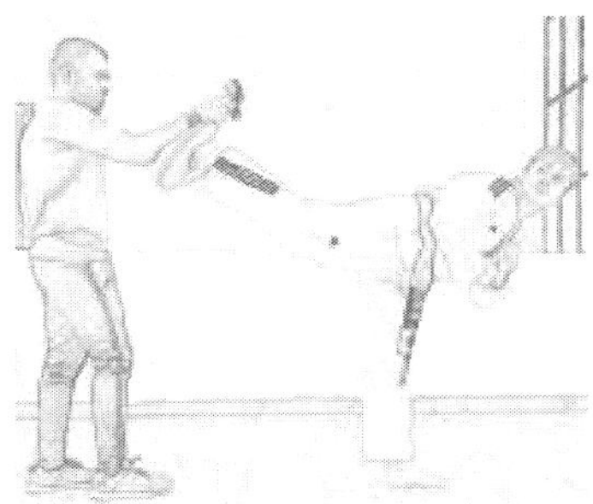

Back kick on pad – 5

Outer edge kick on pad – 6

Inner edge kick on pad -7

Down heel kick on pad -8

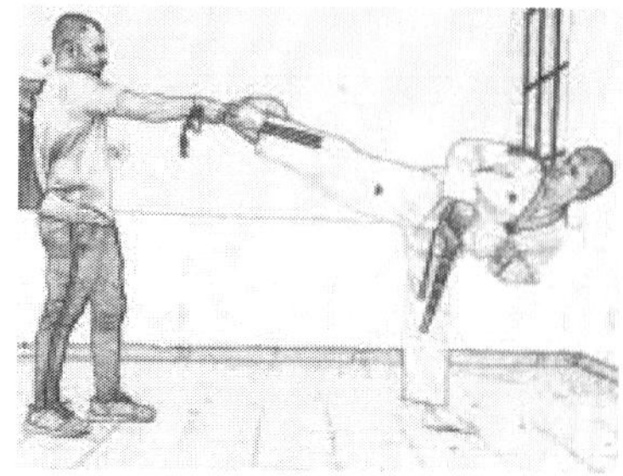

Hook kick on pad – 9

Jumping side kick on pad – 10

Jumping Round house kick on pad - 11

Jumping Back kick on pad – 12

Jumping spin kick on pad - 13

Front Side kick -14

Scissor kick-15

II. PAD KICKING LEFT LEG 40 KICKS IN 30 SECONDS SINGLE LEG

III. PAD KICKING RIGHT LEG 40 KICKS IN 30 SECONDS SINGLE LEG

Note: I,II and III Rest for 1 ½ minutes of each kick, Do all kicks accordingly

Thursday: Same as on Tuesday Schedule

SPEED NYLON / TUBE KICKING

Wednesday 7th week schedule

Speed Kicking With Tube

Tie bicycle tube or nylon thread and tie to your ankle and kick all kicks 40 times in 45 seconds alternative leg. Rest for 1 minute with each kick.
Do all kicks below mentioned stationary kicks 40 kicks in 40 seconds and 20 jumping kicks in 50 seconds.

Speed Kicking With Tube

Tie bicycle tube or nylon thread and tie to your ankle and kick all kicks 40 times with each leg. This improves kicking speed. Once in a week you can do single leg kick and alternative leg kicks.

Side Kick with Left

Side Kick with Right

Hook

Outer edge kick

Round house kick

Thrust kick

Back kick

Back kick

Jumping Round house kick

Jumping side kick with Right leg

Jumping side kick with Left leg

SPEED KICKING ON PAD WITH TIEING TUBE

Down heel kick with tube

Inner edge kick with tube

Outer edge kick with tube

Front thrust kick with tube

Round house kick with tube

Side kick with tube

Back kick with tube

Hook kick with tube

Jumping Round house kick with tube

Jumping Back kick with tube

Jumping side kick with tube

Jumping thrust kick with tube

Turning Jumping Round house
kick with tube Pic -A1

Turning Jumping Round house
kick with tube pic-A2

Turning Jumping Round house kick
with tube Pic -A3

WEDNESDAY: **SPEED TRAINING OF PUNCHES**

7th week schedule

(vii) Knuckle pushups, Close fist and keep knuckle on ground with shoulder width distance and go down and come up. Do 35 pushups and 175 punches in 1 minute. See pictures A and B and C

Pic - AA

Pic- C

Pic - B

(ii) Single hand knuckle pushups: Do one hand knuckle pushups 20 times one hand 45 punches in 1 minute and Change knuckles. Do alternate hands Do 2 sets. See picture A

Pic - A

(iii) Power pushups for speed & power punches

Sit on kneeling position with palms facing ground and jump forward onto your palms on the floor as shown in pictures A and B. Do 5 sets and get up and Do 250 punches in 3 minutes.

Pic –A

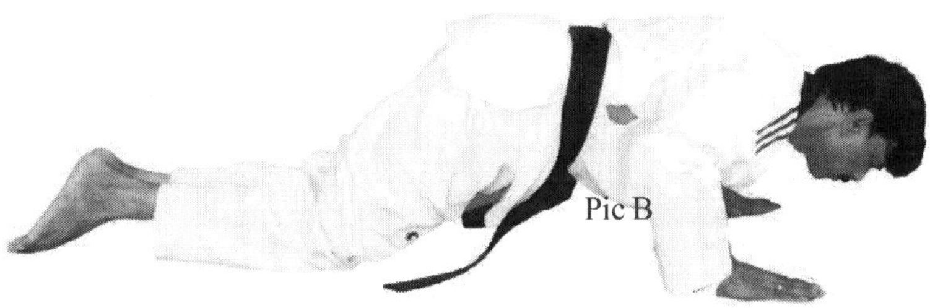

Pic B

(iv) Pushing the kit bag and speed punch exercise: pushing the kit bag and 2 hands punches alternatively .Do 45 sets See pic- P1, P2 and P3

Pic –P1

Pic –P2

Pic –P3

Saturday: <u>Tube kicking with single leg</u>

7th week schedule

Tube kicking with single leg 45 kicks in 45 seconds one minute Rest between each single leg kicks

Do all kicks 45 times in 45 seconds each leg. Below mentioned kicks.

Side Kick with Left

Side Kick with Right

Hook

Outer edge kick

Round house kick

Thrust kick

Back kick

Back kick

Jumping Round house kick

SPEED UNDER WATER KICKS & UNDER WATER PUNCHES

Sunday 7th week schedule, water workout (water must be chest level)

I. Under water kicks Do 1 to 8 kicks each leg 20 kicks (total 40 kicks) in 1 minute

1.Inner edge kick

2.Thrust kick

3.Side kick

4.Spinning kick

5.Round house kick

6. Hook kick

7. Outer edge kick

8. Hook kick and side kick with holding wall

II. a. Running in the water :
Running in the water 25 meters

b. Side Running in the water :
Running in the water right side 25 meters and left side 25 meters

c. knee raising in the water :
Knee raising in the water each leg 50 times (Total 100 times)

d. punches in the water :
(i) 175 double punches in the water with alternative hands
(ii) 125 single hands punches with the left hand and right hand (Total 250 punches)

e. check the speed of every individual kicks in 1 minute and make a of table improvement (minimum kicks must be 180 kicks in 1 minute)

f. check the speed of every individual kicks in 1 minute and make a of table improvement

SQUATS KICKS

Sunday Body Weight Squats Kicks below following kicks

7th week schedule

Sit on squat and get up and kick Down heel kick with one squat 2 kicks the Right leg and left leg and sit. Do 20 kicks each leg (i.e. Total 40 kicks) See pic-L1,pic-L2,pic-L3 and pic-4

Pic-L1

Pic-L2

Pic-L3

Pic-L4

Sit on squat and get up and kick inner edge with Right leg and left leg and sit. Do 20 kicks each leg (i.e. Total 40 kicks) see pic- L5 and pic-L6.

Sit on squat and get up and kick outer edge with left leg and Right leg and sit. Do 20 kicks each leg (i.e. Total 40 kicks) See pic- L7 and pic-L8.

Sit on squat and get up and kick front thrust kick with Right leg and with the Left leg and sit. Do 20 kicks each leg (i.e. Total 40 kicks) See pic-L9 and pic-L10

Pic-L5

Pic-L6

Pic-L7

Pic-L8

Pic-L9

Pic-L10

Sit on squat and get up and kick side kick with Right leg and with the Left leg and sit. Do 20 kicks each leg (i.e. Total 40 kicks) See pic-L11 and pic-L12.

Sit on squat and get up and kick front side kick with Right leg and with the Left leg and sit. Do 20 kicks each leg (i.e. Total 40 kicks) See pic-L13 and pic-L14.

Sit on squat and get up and kick Round house kick with Left leg and with the Right leg and sit. Do 20 kicks each leg (i.e. Total 40 kicks) See pic-L15 and pic-L16.

Pic-L11

Pic-L12

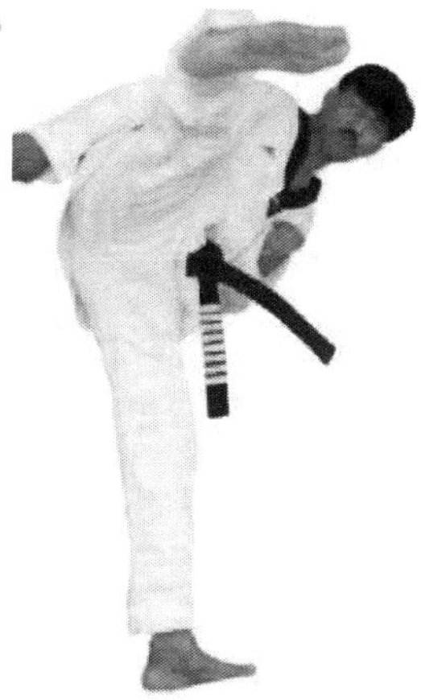

Pic-L13

Pic-L14

Pic-L15

Pic-L16 (side view)

Sit on squat and get up and kick Back kick with Right leg and with the Left leg and sit. Do 20 kicks each leg (i.e. Total 40 kicks) See pic-L17, pic-L18 and L19 Back kick in Front View.

Pic-L17

Pic-L18

Back kick Front view Pic-L19

Sit on squat and get up and kick Hook kick with Left leg and with the Right leg and sit. Do 20 kicks each leg (i.e. Total 40 kicks) See pic-L20, pic-L21 Front view.

Pic-L20 (Side View)

Hook kick front viewPic-L21

SPEED TRAINING OF KICKS-13 TO 15 YEARS

Monday –I 7th week schedule

1kg ANKLE (LEG) WEIGHTS KICKS(Alternative Legs)

Wear a Ankle weight to your leg 1 kg each leg and start kicking all the kicks as shown in the pictures below. Each kick you need to do a minimum of 55kicks each leg in 1 minute Rest for 2 minute. Do all 1 to 10 kicks.

1. down heel kick, alternative legs
2. Side Kick, alternative Legs
3. Spinning cart wheel kick, alternative legs
4. Hook Kick, alternative Legs
5. Trust Kick alternative Leg
6. Inner edge kicks alternative legs
7. Front side kicks alternative legs
8. Round House Kick Alternative Legs
9. Outer Edge Kick Alternative Legs
10. Back Kick and Do Alternative Leg

II. 1kgs of Ankle Weight kick Controlling:

Do only 4 Kicks i.e., (1) Thrust Kick (2) Side Kick (3) Round House Kick (4) Back Kick

Control Each Leg at hips minimum do control for 30 to 35 seconds without any support.

III. Sitting kicks with 1 kg Ankle Weight:

Do only 4 kicks (1) snap kicks (2) Side kick (3) Round house kick (4) Hook kick.
Do each kick 90 times alternative legs Lie down on back and wear 1kgs Ankle weight and kick continuously snap kicks for 90 kicks

Kneel Led down and sit and hands support on the ground and raise your Right leg Right side and kick side kick continuously 45 kicks with wearing 1kg Ankle weights and change the leg and do with other leg same.

Kneel down and sit and hands support on the ground and kick round house kick sideways 45 times each leg with wearing 1kgs Ankle weight.

Kneel down and sit and hands support on the ground and kick Hook kick sideways 45 times each leg wearing 1kg Ankle weight

SPEED TRAINING OF PUNCHES - 13 TO 15 YEARS

Monday –I 7th week schedule

½ kg HAND WEIGHTS (Alternative Hands)

(a) Horse stand and hold ½ kg hand weight and Do 75 punches with alternative hands in 1 minute

(b) Stand in front forward stance and punch with single Right hand over the left open hand (Bend at elbow in the front) 35 punches with Single hand with ½ kg hand weight in 1 minute
And change the hand i.e. change to left hand and punch with the same as Right hand punch.

(C) Speed sitting hand weights punches Sit on chair or stool and punch at least 55 times with alternative hand (with left hand and right hand)
Variation: your can do this sitting punches by blind folded i.e. with closing eyes, by imagining you are smashing with punch.

(d) Forearm Exercise
Forearm and wrist strengthening
Stand with holding one sided dumbbell 8 pounds (approximately) sideways should be besides you and pull up as high as possible, Front side. Do with left hand and with right hand. This exercise will strengthen wrist, forearm.

(e) Forearm Strengthening Exercise
Stand with holding one sided dumbbell 8 pounds (approximately) with right hand beside your thigh and pull up and down back side 18 times each hand alternately.

(f) Wrist Strengthening Exercises
Sit on chair and hold one side dumbbell 8 pounds (approximately) with Right forearm on the thighs and twist to left and right side with maximum strain. Do with other hand, Do 13 times each.

(g) Forearm Strengthening
Sit on stool and holding bar with 15 pounds (approximately) weight with palm facing sky, as shown in picture with hands 10" inches apart and pull up your wrist to you and pull down 18 times. Note: Keep forearm and elbow on the thighs to balance the weight

(h) Forearm strengthening
Sit on stool and holding bar15 pounds (approximately) as shown in picture with hands 10" inches apart and pull to you and pull down 15 times. Note: Keep forearm and elbow on the thighs to balance the weight with palm facing floor in punching position

(i)Forearm Strengthening Exercises 11
Holding 12" to 15" long rod 8 pounds (approximately) tightly on the right side and twist 180degrees for 25 times and change the hand and continue.
Variations: You can hold 2 rods either side of each hand and twist them.

(j)Forearm Strengthening
Hold 12" to 14" rod 8 pounds (approximately) in front of you and twist left and right 180 degrees angle with left hand 20 to 25 repetitions and change to right hand and do the same repetitions.

(k) Triceps Strengthening Exercise
Keep index and thumb of each hand join together and go for pushups with leg stretch out without bending knees. Do this exercise for 10 to 15 times daily.

Friday: Same as on Monday Schedule

SPEED PEDDLE KICKS(kicking on pad)

Tuesday 7th week schedule

I. PAD KICKING EACH LEG 35 KICKS 1 TO 15 KICKS

(1) Push kick

(2) Front thrust kick

(3) Side kick

(4) Round house kick

(5) Back kick

(6) Outer edge kick

(7) Inner edge kick

(8) Down heel kick

(9) Hook kick

(10) Jumping side kick

(11) Jumping Round house kick

(12) Jumping Back kick

(13) Spin kick

(14) Jumping spin kick

(15) Scissor kick

II. PAD KICKING LEFT LEG 35 KICKS IN 30 SECONDS SINGLE LEG

III. PAD KICKING RIGHT LEG 35 KICKS IN 30 SECONDS SINGLE LEG

Note: I,II and III Rest for 1 ½ minutes of each kick, Do all kicks accordingly

Thursday: Same as on Tuesday Schedule

SPEED NYLON / TUBE KICKING

Wednesday 7th week schedule

Speed Kicking With Tube

Tie bicycle tube or nylon thread and tie to your ankle and kick all kicks 35 times in 45 seconds alternative leg. Rest for 1 minute with each kick in air or kicking pad.
Do all kicks below mentioned stationary kicks 35 kicks in 45 seconds and 18 jumping kicks in 50 seconds.

Speed Kicking With Tube

Tie bicycle tube or nylon thread and tie to your ankle and kick all kicks 35 times with each leg.

This improves kicking speed. Once in a week you can do single leg kick and alternative leg kicks.

Do below mentioned kicks.

1. Side Kick with Left and Right Leg
2. Outer edge kick with Left and Right Leg
3. Inner edge kick with Left and Right Leg
4. Thrust kick with Left and Right Leg
5. Back kick with Left and Right Leg
6. Round house kick with Left and Right Leg
7. Hook Kick with Left and Right Leg
8. Jumping Round house kick with Left and Right Leg
9. Jumping side kick with Left and Right Leg
10. Down heel kick with Left and Right Leg
11. Jumping Thrust kick with Left and Right Leg
12. Jumping Back kick with Left and Right Leg

WEDNESDAY: SPEED TRAINING OF PUNCHES

7th week schedule

(i) Knuckle pushups, Close fist and keep knuckle on ground with shoulder width distance and go down and come up. Do 25 push ups and 90 punches in 1 minute.

(ii) Single hand knuckle pushups: Do one hand knuckle pushups 13 times one hand 25 punches in 1 minute and Change knuckles. Do alternate hands Do 2 sets

(iii) Power pushups for speed & power punches
Sit on kneeling position with palms facing ground and jump forward onto your palms on the Floor and Do 4 sets and get up and Do 175 punches in 2 minutes.

(iv) Pushing the kit bag and speed punch exercise: pushing the kit bag and 2 hands punches alternatively .Do 35 sets

Saturday: Tube kicking with single leg

7th week schedule

Tube kicking with single leg 35 kicks in 45 seconds one minute or 2 minutes Rest between each single leg kicks

Do all kicks 35 times in 45 seconds each leg. Below mentioned kicks.

1. Side Kick with Left and Right Leg
2. Hook Kick with Left and Right Leg
3. Outer edge kick with Left and Right Leg
4. Round house kick with Left and Right Leg
5. *Thrust kick* with Left and Right Leg
6. Back kick with Left and Right Leg
7. Jumping Round house kick with Left and Right Leg
8. Inner edge kick with Left and Right Leg

SPEED UNDER WATER KICKS & UNDER WATER PUNCHES

Sunday 7th week schedule, water workout (water must be chest level)

I. Under water kicks Do 1 to 8 kicks each leg 12 kicks (total 24 kicks) in 1 minute
Do below mentioned kicks

1. Inner edge kick
2. Thrust kick
3. Side kick
4. Spinning kick
5. Round house kick
6. Hook kick
7. Outer edge kick
8. Hook kick and side kick with holding wall

II. a. Running in the water :
Running in the water 25 meters

b. Side Running in the water :
Running in the water right side 25 meters and left side 25 meters

c. knee raising in the water :
Knee raising in the water each leg 50 times (Total 100 times)

d. punches in the water :
(i)135 double punches in the water with alternative hands
(ii)90 single hands punches with the left hand and right hand (Total 180 punches)

e. check the speed of every individual kicks in 1 minute and make a table of improvement (minimum kicks must be 180 kicks in 1 minute in Air every week)

SQUATS KICKS

Sunday Body Weight Squats Kicks below following kicks 7th week schedule

Sit on squat and get up and kick Down heel kick with one squat 2 kicks with the Right leg and left leg and sit. Do 18 kicks each leg (i.e. Total 40 kicks)

Sit on squat and get up and kick inner edge with Right leg and left leg and sit. Do 18 kicks each leg (i.e. Total 36 kicks.

Sit on squat and get up and kick outer edge with left leg and Right leg and sit. Do 18 kicks each leg (i.e. Total 36 kicks).

Sit on squat and get up and kick front thrust kick with Right leg and with the Left leg and sit. Do 18 kicks each leg (i.e. Total 36 kicks) .

Sit on squat and get up and kick side kick with Right leg and with the Left leg and sit. Do 18 kicks each leg (i.e. Total 36 kicks).

Sit on squat and get up and kick front side kick with Right leg and with the Left leg and sit. Do 18 kicks each leg (i.e. Total 36 kicks).

Sit on squat and get up and kick Round house kick with Left leg and with the Right leg and sit. Do 18 kicks each leg (i.e. Total 36 kicks).

Sit on squat and get up and kick Back kick with Right leg and with the Left leg and sit. Do 18 kicks each leg (i.e. Total 36 kicks).

Sit on squat and get up and kick Hook kick with Left leg and with the Right leg and sit. Do 18 kicks each leg (i.e. Total 36 kicks).

SPEED TRAINING OF KICKS - BELOW 13 YEARS

Monday –I 6th & 7th week schedule

110 KICKS IN 2 MINITUES

Each kick you need to do a minimum of 55 kicks each leg in 1 minute Rest for 2 minute. Do all 1 to 10 kicks. Below mention kicks

1. down heel kick, alternative legs
2. Side Kick, alternative Legs
3. Spinning cart wheel kick, alternative legs
4. Hook Kick, alternative Legs
5. Trust Kick alternative Leg
6. Inner edge kicks alternative legs
7. Front side kicks alternative legs
8. Round House Kick Alternative Legs
9. Outer Edge Kick Alternative Legs
10. Back Kick and Do Alternative Leg

II. kick Controlling:

Do only 4 Kicks i.e., (1) Thrust Kick (2) Side Kick (3) Round House Kick (4) BackKick

Control Each Leg at hips minimum do control for 30 to 35 seconds without any support.

III. Sitting kicks :

Do only 4 kicks (1) snap kicks (2) Side kick (3) Round house kick (4) Hook kick.
Do each kick 90 times alternative legs Lie down on back and kick continuously snap kicks start from 45 kicks to 90 kicks

Kneel Led down and sit and hands support on the ground and raise your Right leg Right side and kick side kick continuously 45 to 90 and change the leg and do with other leg same.

Kneel down and sit and hands support on the ground and kick round house kick sideways 45 to 90 times each leg.

Kneel down and sit and hands support on the ground and kick Hook kick sideways 45 to 90 times each leg.

Variation : kicks on x-ray film. You can do all kicks and all punches on x-ray film each kick 18 times and 90 punch with 2 hands.

SPEED TRAINING OF PUNCHES - BELOW 13 YEARS

Monday –I 6th & 7th week schedule

160 punches in 1 minute (Alternative Hands)

(a) Horse stand and Do 160 punches with alternative hands in 1 minute Do 2 sets.

(b) Stand in front forward stance and punch with single Right hand over the left open hand (Bend at elbow in the front) 90 punches with Single hand with in 1 minute Do 2 sets And change the hand i.e. change to left hand and punch with the same as Right hand punch.

(C) Speed sitting hand punches Sit on chair or stool and punch at least 125 times with alternative hand (with left hand and right hand) Do 2 sets.
Variation: your can do this sitting punches by blind folded i.e. with closing eyes, by imagining you are smashing with punch.

(d) Punches on x-ray film: you can practices 90 with each hand (total 180 punches)

(e) Triceps Strengthening Exercise
Keep index and thumb of each hand join together and go for pushups with leg stretch out without bending knees. Do this exercise for 10 to 15 times daily.

Friday: Same as on Monday Schedule

SPEED PEDDLE KICKS(kicking on pad)

Tuesday 6th &7th week schedule

I. PAD KICKING EACH LEG 35 KICKS 1 TO 15 KICKS

(1) Push kick - 35 kicks each leg
(2) Front thrust kick " "
(3) Side kick " "
(4) Round house kick " "
(5) Back kick " "
(6) Outer edge kick " "
(7) Inner edge kick " "
(8) Down heel kick " "
(9) Hook kick " "
(10) Jumping side kick " "
(11) Jumping Round house kick " "

(12) Jumping Back kick - 25 kicks each leg

(13) Spin kick -35 kicks each leg

(14) Jumping spin kick -25 kicks each leg

(15) Scissor kick - 35 kicks each leg

II. PAD KICKING LEFT LEG 35 KICKS IN 1MINITE SINGLE LEG

III. PAD KICKING RIGHT LEG 35 KICKS IN 1MINITE SINGLE LEG

Note: I,II and III Rest for 1 ½ minutes of each kick, Do all kicks accordingly

Thursday: Same as on Tuesday Schedule

WEDNESDAY: SPEED TRAINING OF PUNCHES

$6^{th\ \&\ 7th}$ week schedule

(i) Knuckle pushups, Close fist and keep knuckle on ground with shoulder width distance and go down and come up or palms pushups Do 15 pushups and 90 punches in 1 minute.

(ii) Single hand knuckle or palms pushups: Do one hand knuckle pushups 15 times one hand 50 punches in 1 minute and Change knuckles. Do alternate hands Do 2 sets

(iii) Power pushups for speed & power punches
Sit on kneeling position with palms facing ground and jump forward onto your palms on the Floor and Do 3 sets and get up and Do 180 punches in 3 minutes.

(iv) Pushing the kit bag and speed punch exercise: pushing the kit bag and 2 hands punches alternatively .Do 35 sets

SPEED UNDER WATER KICKS & UNDER WATER PUNCHES

Sunday $6^{th\ \&\ 7\ th}$ week schedule, water workout (water must be chest level)

I. Under water kicks Do 1 to 8 kicks each leg 12 kicks (total 24 kicks) in 1 minute
Do below mentioned kicks

1.Inner edge kick

2.Thrust kick

3.Side kick

4.Spinning kick

5.Round house kick

6. Hook kick

7. Outer edge kick

8. Hook kick and side kick with holding wall

II. a. Running in the water :
Running in the water 15 meters

b. Side Running in the water :
Running in the water right side 15 meters and left side 15 meters

c. knee raising in the water :
Knee raising in the water each leg 35 times (Total 70 times)

d. punches in the water :
(i) 90 double punches in the water with alternative hands
(ii)65 single hands punches with the left hand and right hand (Total 130 punches)

e. check every week the speed of every individual kicks in 1 minute and make a table of improvement (minimum kicks must be 160 kicks in 1 minute in Air every week)

SQUATS KICKS

Sunday Body Weight Squats Kicks below following kicks
6th & 7th week schedule

Sit on squat and get up and kick Down heel kick with one squat 2 kicks with the Right leg and left leg and sit. Do 12 kicks each leg (i.e. Total 24 kicks) in 1 minute.

Sit on squat and get up and kick inner edge with Right leg and left leg and sit. Do 12 kicks each leg (i.e. Total 24 kicks) in 1 minute.

Sit on squat and get up and kick outer edge with left leg and Right leg and sit. Do 12 kicks each leg (i.e. Total 24 kicks) in 1 minute.

Sit on squat and get up and kick front thrust kick with Right leg and with the Left leg and sit. Do 12 kicks each leg (i.e. Total 24 kicks) in 1 minute.

Sit on squat and get up and kick side kick with Right leg and with the Left leg and sit. Do 12 kicks each leg (i.e. Total 24 kicks) in 1 minute.

Sit on squat and get up and kick front side kick with Right leg and with the Left leg and sit. Do 12 kicks each leg (i.e. Total 24 kicks) in 1 minute.

Sit on squat and get up and kick Round house kick with Left leg and with the Right leg and sit. Do 12 kicks each leg (i.e. Total 24 kicks) in 1 minute.

Sit on squat and get up and kick Back kick with Right leg and with the Left leg and sit. Do 12 kicks each leg (i.e. Total 24 kicks) in 1 minute.

Sit on squat and get up and kick Hook kick with Left leg and with the Right leg and sit. Do 12 kicks each leg (i.e. Total 24 kicks) in 1 minute.

8^Th^ Week

Th

8

Speed Training schedule for 15 Years and above

Speed Training schedule for 13 – 15 Years

Speed Training schedule for below 13 years

Week

"Don't worry about how slowly you are improving, as long as you don't stop. You can see one day speed proceed it"

- Grand Master M. Jayanth Reddy

SPEED TRAINING OF KICKS- 15 YEAR AND ABOVE

Monday –I 8th week schedule

2kgs ANKLE (LEG) WEIGHTS KICKS(Alternative Legs)

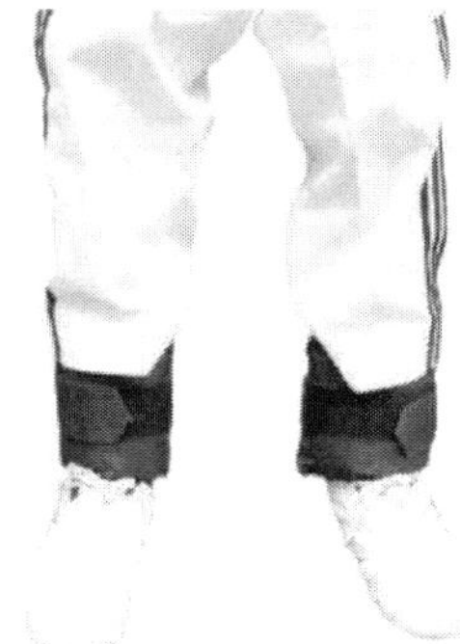

Wear a Ankle weight to your leg 2 kg each leg and start kicking all the kicks as shown in the pictures below. Each kick you need to do a minimum of 60 kicks each leg in 1 minute Rest for 2 minute. Do all 1 to 10 kicks.

1.DOWN HEEL KICK, ALTERNATIVE LEGS

2.SIDE KICK, ALTERNATIVE LEGS

3.SPINNING CART WHEEL KICK, ALTERNATIVE LEGS

4.HOOK KICK, ALTERNATIVE LEGS

5.TRUST KICK ALTENATIVE LEG

6. INNER EDGE KICKS ALTERNATIVE LEGS

7. FRONT SIDE KICKS ALTERNATIVE LEGS

8. ROUND HOUSE KICK ALTERNATIVE LEGS

9. OUTER EDGE KICK ALTERNATIVE LEGS

10. BACK KICK AND DO ALTERNATIVE LEG

II. 2kgs of Ankle Weight kick Controlling:

Do only 4 Kicks i.e., (1) Thrust Kick (2) Side Kick (3) Round House Kick (4) Back Kick Control Each Leg at hips minimum do control for 30 to 45 seconds without any support. See Picture A,B,C and D. Do 2 sets each.

Pic-A

Thrust Kick, Alternative Legs

Pic-B

Side Kick, Alternative

Pic-C

Round House Kick Alternative

Pic-D

Back Kick do with Alternative Leg

III. Sitting kicks with 2 kgs Ankle weight :

Do only 4 kicks (1) snap kicks (2) Side kick (3) Round house kick (4) Hook kick.
Do each kick 150 times alternative legs Lie down on back and wear 2 kgs Ankle weight and kick continuously snap kicks for 50 to 100 kicks see pic-P1 ,pic- P2 and p3.

Pic-P1

Pic-P2

Pic-P3

Kneel led down and sit and hands support on the ground and raise your Right leg Right side and kick side kick continuously 50 to 100 kicks with wearing 2kg Ankle weights and change the leg and do with other leg same. See pic-P4 and pic-P5.

Pic-P4

pic-P5

Kneel led down and sit and hands support on the ground and kick round house kick sideways 50 to 100 times each leg with wearing 2kgs Ankle weight. See pic-P6 and pic-P7

Pic-P6

Pic-P7

Kneel led down and sit and hands support on the ground and kick Hook kick sideways 50 to 100 times each leg wearing 2kgs Ankle weight. See pic-P8 and pic-P9.

pic-P8

pic-P9

SPEED TRAINING OF PUNCHES - 15 YEAR AND ABOVE

Monday –I 8th week schedule

1kgs HAND WEIGHTS (Alternative Hands)

(a) Horse stand and hold 1 kg hand weight and Do 120 punches with alternative hands in 1 minute See picture 1 and 2

Pic -1

Pic -2

(b) Stand in front forward stance and punch with single Right hand over the left open hand (Bend at elbow in the front) 70 punches with Single hand with 1kg hand weight in 1 minute

And change the hand i.e. change to left hand And punch with the same as Right hand punch. See picture 3,4,5 and 6

Pic -3

Pic -4

Pic -5

Pic -6

(C) Speed sitting hand weights punches Sit on chair or stool and punch at least 100 times with alternative hand (with left hand and right hand)

Variation: your can do this sitting punches by blind folded i.e. with closing eyes, by imagining you are smashing with punch. See picture 7 and 8

Pic -7

Pic -8

(D) Biceps Forearm Triceps Strengthening Exercises for Speed

Bicep Exercise 1

Hold 10 pounds in left hand and pull till chest. This will strengthen the biceps. Do with other hand each 3 sets of 20 times. Refer pictures A, B , A1 and B1

Pic -A

Pic -B

Pic -A1

Pic - B1

Bicep Exercise 2

Sit on chair and take 15 pounds hand dumbbell and pull up to chest level 20 repetitions each hand alternatively. Refer pictures A, B, C and D.

Pic -A

Pic -B

Pic -B

Pic -D

Triceps Strengthening 3

Horse stance with barbell weight back of you and slightly bend forward your upper body and lift weight 15 pounds. See picture A.

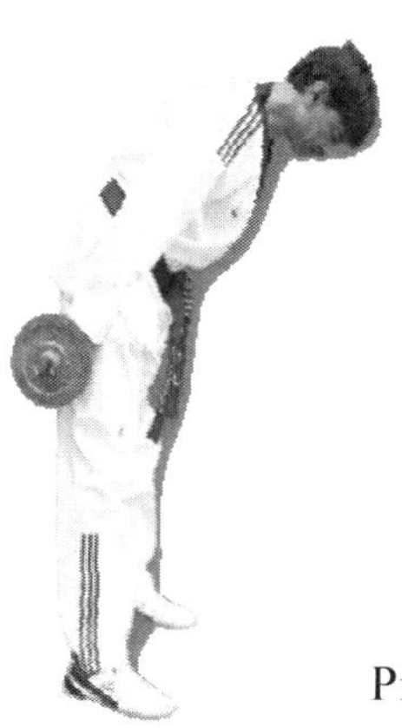

Pic - A

Biceps Strengthening 4

Stand with barbell weight on your hand forward pull weight up to chest and withdraw to thighs. Do with 20 pounds increases according to your capacity. Do at least 20 repetitions Do 3 sets. . See picture A.

Pic -A

Forearm Exercise 5

Forearm and wrist strengthening

Stand with holding one sided dumbbell 8 pounds (approximately) sideways should be besides you and pull up as high as possible, Front side. Do with left hand and with right hand. This exercise will strengthen wrist, forearm. See pictures A, B, A1 and B1.

Pic - A

Pic - B

Pic – A1

Pic – B1

Forearm Strengthening Exercise 6

Stand with holding one sided dumbbell 8 pounds (approximately) with right hand beside your thigh and pull up and down back side 20 times each hand alternately. See picture C and D.

Pic - C

Pic - D

Wrist Strengthening Exercises7

Sit on chair and hold one side dumbbell 8 pounds (approximately) with Right forearm on the thighs and twist to left and right side with maximum strain. Do with other hand, Do 15 times each. See pictures A, B, C, D, E, F

Pic -A

Pic - B

Pic - C

Pic -D

Pic - E

Pic - F

Triceps Exercise 8

Sit on chair and hold one side Drum bell 8 to 10 pounds (approximately) with Right hand Back side and pull up and Down, See pictures S1, S2, S3, and S4

Pic – S1

Pic – S2

Pic – S3

Pic – S4

Forearm Strengthening 9

Sit on stool and holding bar with 15 pounds (approximately) weight with palm facing sky, as shown in picture with hands 10" inches apart and pull up your wrist to you and pull down 20 times. Note: Keep forearm and elbow on the thighs to balance the weight. See pictures A and B.

Pic – A

Pic - B

Forearm strengthening 10

Sit on stool and holding bar15 pounds (approximately) as shown in picture with hands 10" inches apart and pull to you and pull down 20 times. Note: Keep forearm and elbow on the thighs to balance the weight with palm facing floor in punching position. See pictures C and D.

Pic – C

Pic – D

Forearm Strengthening Exercises 11

Holding 12" to 15" long rod 8 pounds (approximately) tightly on the right side and twist 180degrees for 30 times and change the hand and continue. See pictures A, B, C

Variations: You can hold 2 rods either side of each hand and twist them.

Pic - A

Pic - B

Pic - C

Forearm Strengthening 12

Hold 12" to 14" rod 8 pounds (approximately) in front of you and twist left and right 180 degrees angle with left hand 20 to 30 repetitions and change to right hand and do the same repetitions. See pictures A, B, C, D, E and F.

Pic - A Pic – B Pic – C Pic- D Pic – E Pic - F

Triceps Strengthening Exercise 13

Keep index and thumb of each hand join together and go for pushups with leg stretch out without bending knees. Do this exercise for 10 to 20 times daily. See pictures A and B.

Pic A

Pic B

Friday: Same as on Monday Schedule

SPEED PEDDLE KICKS(kicking on pad)

Tuesday 8th week schedule

I. PAD KICKING EACH LEG 50 KICKS 1 TO 15 KICKS

(1) Push kick
(2) Front thrust kick
(3) Side kick
(4) Round house kick
(5) Back kick
(6) Outer edge kick
(7) Inner edge kick
(8) Down heel kick
(9) Hook kick
(10) Jumping side kick
(11) Jumping Round house kick
(12) Jumping Back kick
(13) Spin kick
(14) Jumping spin kick
(15) Scissor kick

Jumping thrust kick

Push Kick on Pad -1

Front thrust kick on pad -2

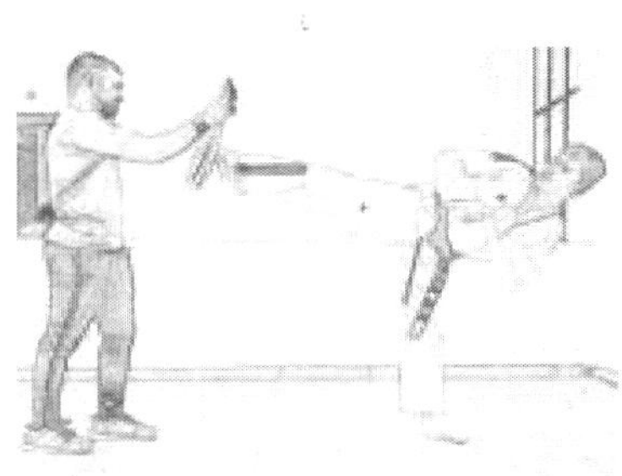

Side kick on pad -3

Round house on pad-4

Back kick on pad – 5

Outer edge kick on pad – 6

Inner edge kick on pad -7

Down heel kick on pad -8

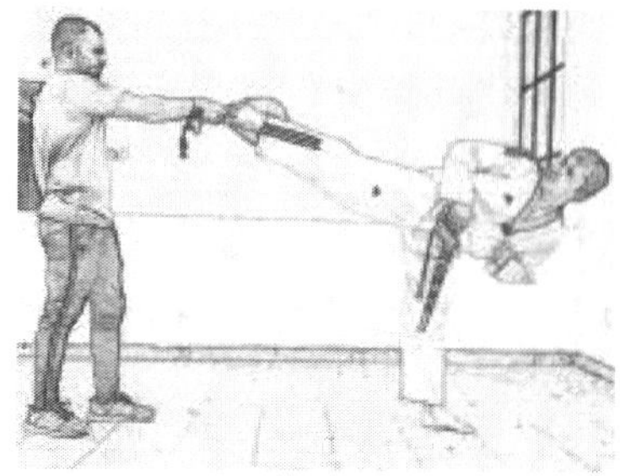

Hook kick on pad – 9

Jumping side kick on pad – 10

Jumping Round house kick on pad - 11

Jumping Back kick on pad – 12

Jumping spin kick on pad - 13

Front Side kick -14

Scissor kick-15

II. PAD KICKING LEFT LEG 50 KICKS IN 30 SECONDS SINGLE LEG

III. PAD KICKING RIGHT LEG 50 KICKS IN 30 SECONDS SINGLE LEG

Note: I,II and III Rest for 1 ½ minutes of each kick, Do all kicks accordingly

Thursday: Same as on Tuesday Schedule

<u>**SPEED NYLON / TUBE KICKING**</u>

Wednesday 8th week schedule

Speed Kicking With Tube

Tie bicycle tube or nylon thread and tie to your ankle and kick all kicks 50 times in 45 seconds alternative leg. Rest for 1 minute with each kick in Air or kicking pad.
Do all kicks below mentioned stationary kicks 50 kicks in 45 seconds and 25 jumping kicks in 50 seconds.

Speed Kicking With Tube

Tie bicycle tube or nylon thread and tie to your ankle and kick all kicks 50 times with each leg.
This improves kicking speed. Once in a week you can do single leg kick and alternative leg kicks.

Side Kick with Left

Side Kick with Right

Hook

Outer edge kick

Round house kick

Thrust kick

Back kick

Back kick

Jumping Round house kick

Jumping side kick with Right leg

Jumping side kick with Left leg

SPEED KICKING ON PAD WITH TIEING TUBE

Down heel kick with tube

Inner edge kick with tube

Outer edge kick with tube

Front thrust kick with tube

Round house kick with tube

Side kick with tube

Back kick with tube

Hook kick with tube

Jumping Round house kick with tube

Jumping Back kick with tube

Jumping side kick with tube

Jumping thrust kick with tube

Turning Jumping Round house
kick with tube Pic -A1

Turning Jumping Round house
kick with tube pic-A2

Turning Jumping Round house kick
with tube Pic -A3

WEDNESDAY: <u>SPEED TRAINING OF PUNCHES</u>

8th week schedule

(i) Knuckle pushups, Close fist and keep knuckle on ground with shoulder width distance and go down and come up. Do 40 push ups and 200 punches in 1 minute. See pictures A and B and C

Pic - A

Pic- C

Pic - B

(ii) Single hand knuckle pushups: Do one hand knuckle pushups 20 times one hand 50 punches in 1 minute and Change knuckles. Do alternate hands Do 2 sets. See picture A

Pic - A

(iii) Power pushups for speed & power punches

Sit on kneeling position with palms facing ground and jump forward onto your palms on the floor as shown in pictures A and B. Do 5 sets and get up and Do 300 punches in 3 minutes.

Pic-A

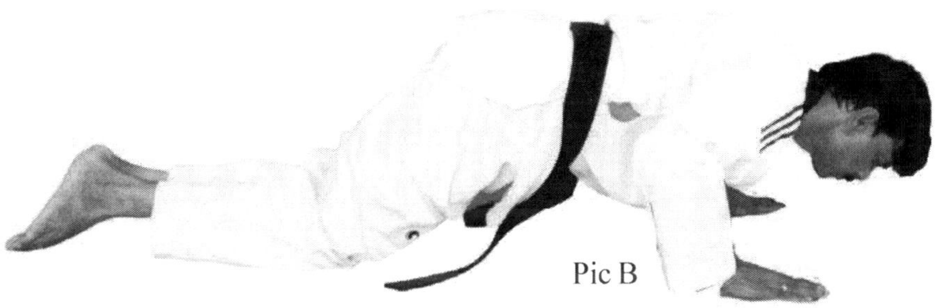

Pic B

(iv) Pushing the kit bag and speed punch exercise: pushing the kit bag and 2 hands punches alternatively .Do 50 sets See pic- P1, P2 and P3

Pic –P1

Pic –P2

Pic P3

Saturday: Tube kicking with single leg

8th week schedule

Tube kicking with single leg 50 kicks in 45 seconds one minute Rest between each single leg kicks

Do all kicks 50 times in 45 seconds each leg. Below mentioned kicks.

Side Kick with Left

Side Kick with Right

Hook

Outer edge kick

Round house kick

Thrust kick

Back kick

Back kick

Jumping Round house kick

SPEED UNDER WATER KICKS & UNDER WATER PUNCHES

Sunday 8th week schedule, water workout (water must be chest level)

I. Under water kicks Do 1 to 8 kicks each leg 20 kicks (total 40 kicks) in 1 minute

1.Inner edge kick

2.Thrust kick

3.Side kick

4.Spinning kick

5.Round house kick

6. Hook kick

7. Outer edge kick

8. Hook kick and side kick with holding wall

II. a. Running in the water :
Running in the water 25 meters

b. Side Running in the water :
Running in the water right side 25 meters and left side 25 meters

c. knee raising in the water :
Knee raising in the water each leg 50 times (Total 100 times)

d. punches in the water :
(i)200 double punches in the water with alternative hands
(ii)150 single hands punches with the left hand and right hand (Total 300 punches)

e. check the speed of every individual kicks in 1 minute and make a table of improvement (minimum kicks must be 180 kicks in 1 minute in Air every week)

SQUATS KICKS

Sunday Body Weight Squats Kicks below following kicks

8th week schedule

Sit on squat and get up and kick Down heel kick with one squat 2 kicks with the Right leg and left leg and sit. Do 25 kicks each leg (i.e. Total 50 kicks) See pic-L1,pic-L2,pic-L3 and pic-4

Pic-L1

Pic-L2

Pic-L3

Pic-L4

Sit on squat and get up and kick inner edge with Right leg and left leg and sit. Do 25 kicks each leg (i.e. Total 50 kicks) see pic- L5 and pic-L6.

Sit on squat and get up and kick outer edge with left leg and Right leg and sit. Do 25 kicks each leg (i.e. Total 50 kicks) See pic- L7 and pic-L8.

Sit on squat and get up and kick front thrust kick with Right leg and with the Left leg and sit. Do 25 kicks each leg (i.e. Total 50 kicks) See pic-L9 and pic-L10

Pic-L5

Pic-L6

Pic-L7

Pic-L8

Pic-L9

Pic-L10

Sit on squat and get up and kick side kick with Right leg and with the Left leg and sit. Do 25 kicks each leg (i.e. Total 50 kicks) See pic-L11 and pic-L12.

Sit on squat and get up and kick front side kick with Right leg and with the Left leg and sit. Do 25 kicks each leg (i.e. Total 50 kicks) See pic-L13 and pic-L14.

Sit on squat and get up and kick Round house kick with Left leg and with the Right leg and sit. Do 25 kicks each leg (i.e. Total 50 kicks) See pic-L15 and pic-L16.

Pic-L11

Pic-L12

Pic-L13

Pic-L14

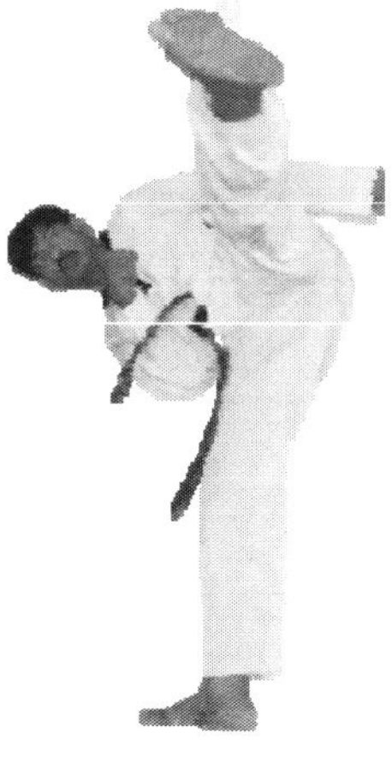
Pic-L15

Pic-L16 (side view)

Sit on squat and get up and kick Back kick with Right leg and with the Left leg and sit. Do 25 kicks each leg (i.e. Total 50 kicks) See pic-L17,pic-L18 and L19 Back kick in Front View.

Pic-L17

Pic-L18

Back kick Front view Pic-L19

Sit on squat and get up and kick Hook kick with Left leg and with the Right leg and sit. Do 25 kicks each leg (i.e. Total 50 kicks) See pic-L20,pic-L21 Front view.

Pic-L20 (Side View)

Hook kick front viewPic-L21

SPEED TRAINING OF KICKS-13 TO 15 YEARS

Monday –I 8th week schedule

1kg ANKLE (LEG) WEIGHTS KICKS(Alternative Legs)

Wear a Ankle weight to your leg 1 kg each leg and start kicking all the kicks as shown in the pictures below. Each kick you need to do a minimum of 60 kicks each leg in 1 minute Rest for 2 minute. Do all 1 to 10 kicks.

1. down heel kick, alternative legs
2. Side Kick, alternative Legs
3. Spinning cart wheel kick, alternative legs
4. Hook Kick, alternative Legs
5. Trust Kick alternative Leg
6. Inner edge kicks alternative legs
7. Front side kicks alternative legs
8. Round House Kick Alternative Legs
9. Outer Edge Kick Alternative Legs
10. Back Kick and Do Alternative Leg

II. 1kgs of Ankle Weight kick Controlling:

Do only 4 Kicks i.e., (1) Thrust Kick (2) Side Kick (3) Round House Kick (4) Back Kick

Control Each Leg at hips minimum do control for 30 to 45 seconds without any support.

III. Sitting kicks with 1 kg Ankle Wight :

Do only 4 kicks (1) snap kicks (2) Side kick (3) Round house kick (4) Hook kick.
Do each kick 100 times alternative legs Lie down on back and wear 1kgs Ankle weight and kick continuously snap kicks for 100 kicks

Kneel Led down and sit and hands support on the ground and raise your Right leg Right side and kick side kick continuously 50 kicks with wearing 1kg Ankle weights and change the leg and do with other leg same.

Kneel down and sit and hands support on the ground and kick round house kick sideways 50 times each leg with wearing 1kgs Ankle weight.

Kneel down and sit and hands support on the ground and kick Hook kick sideways 50 times each leg wearing 1kg Ankle weight

SPEED TRAINING OF PUNCHES - 13 TO 15 YEARS

Monday –I 8th week schedule

½ kg HAND WEIGHTS (Alternative Hands)

(a) Horse stand Horse stand and hold ½ kg hand weight and Do 80 punches with alternative hands in 1 minute

(b) Stand in front forward stance and punch with single Right hand over the left open hand (Bend at elbow in the front) 40 punches with Single hand with ½ kg hand weight in 1 minute And change the hand i.e. change to left hand and punch with the same as Right hand punch.

(c) Speed sitting hand weights punches Sit on chair or stool and punch at least 60 times with alternative hand (with left hand and right hand)

Variation: your can do this sitting punches by blind folded i.e. with closing eyes, by imagining you are smashing with punch.

(d) Forearm Exercise

Forearm and wrist strengthening

Stand with holding one sided dumbbell 8 pounds (approximately) sideways should be besides you and pull up as high as possible, Front side. Do with left hand and with right hand. This exercise will strengthen wrist, forearm.

(e) Forearm Strengthening Exercise

Stand with holding one sided dumbbell 8 pounds (approximately) with right hand beside your thigh and pull up and down back side 20 times each hand alternately.

(f) Wrist Strengthening Exercises

Sit on chair and hold one side dumbbell 8 pounds (approximately) with Right forearm on the thighs and twist to left and right side with maximum strain. Do with other hand, Do 15 times each.

g) Forearm Strengthening

Sit on stool and holding bar with 15 pounds (approximately) weight with palm facing sky, as shown in picture with hands 10" inches apart and pull up your wrist to you and pull down 20 times. Note: Keep forearm and elbow on the thighs to balance the weight

(h) Forearm strengthening

Sit on stool and holding bar15 pounds (approximately) as shown in picture with hands 10" inches apart and pull to you and pull down 20 times. Note: Keep forearm and elbow on the thighs to balance the weight with palm facing floor in punching position

(i)Forearm Strengthening Exercises

Holding 12" to 15" long rod 8 pounds (approximately) tightly on the right side and twist 180degrees for 30 times and change the hand and continue.

Variations: You can hold 2 rods either side of each hand and twist them.

(j)Forearm Strengthening
Hold 12" to 14" rod 8 pounds (approximately) in front of you and twist left and right 180 degrees angle with left hand 20 to 30 repetitions and change to right hand and do the same repetitions.

(k) Triceps Strengthening Exercise
Keep index and thumb of each hand join together and go for pushups with leg stretch out without bending knees. Do this exercise for 10 to 20 times daily.

Friday: Same as on Monday Schedule

SPEED PEDDLE KICKS(kicking on pad)
Tuesday 8th week schedule

I. PAD KICKING EACH LEG 40 KICKS 1 TO 15 KICKS

(1) Push kick

(2) Front thrust kick

(3) Side kick

(4) Round house kick

(5) Back kick

(6) Outer edge kick

(7) Inner edge kick

(8) Down heel kick

(9) Hook kick

(10) Jumping side kick

(11) Jumping Round house kick

(12) Jumping Back kick

(13) Spin kick

(14) Jumping spin kick

(15) Scissor kick

II. PAD KICKING LEFT LEG 40 KICKS IN 30 SECONDS SINGLE LEG

III. PAD KICKING RIGHT LEG 40 KICKS IN 30 SECONDS SINGLE LEG

Note: I,II and III Rest for 1 ½ minutes of each kick, Do all kicks accordingly

Thursday: Same as on Tuesday Schedule

SPEED NYLON / TUBE KICKING

Wednesday 8th week schedule

Speed Kicking With Tube

Tie bicycle tube or nylon thread and tie to your ankle and kick all kicks 40 times in 45 seconds alternative leg. Rest for 1 minute with each kick in air or kicking pad.

Do all kicks below mentioned stationary kicks 40 kicks in 45 seconds and 20 jumping kicks in 50 seconds.

Speed Kicking With Tube

Tie bicycle tube or nylon thread and tie to your ankle and kick all kicks 40 times with each leg.

This improves kicking speed. Once in a week you can do single leg kick and alternative leg kicks.

Do below mentioned kicks.

1. Side Kick with Left and Right Leg
2. Outer edge kick with Left and Right Leg
3. Inner edge kick with Left and Right Leg
4. Thrust kick with Left and Right Leg
5. Back kick with Left and Right Leg
6. Round house kick with Left and Right Leg
7. Hook Kick with Left and Right Leg
8. Jumping Round house kick with Left and Right Leg
9. Jumping side kick with Left and Right Leg
10. Down heel kick with Left and Right Leg
11. Jumping Thrust kick with Left and Right Leg
12. Jumping Back kick with Left and Right Leg

WEDNESDAY: **SPEED TRAINING OF PUNCHES**

8th week schedule

(i) Knuckle pushups, Close fist and keep knuckle on ground with shoulder width distance and go down and come up. Do 30 push ups and 100 punches in 1 minute.

(ii) Single hand knuckle pushups: Do one hand knuckle pushups 15 times one hand 30 punches in 1 minute and Change knuckles. Do alternate hands Do 2 sets

(iii) Power pushups for speed & power punches
Sit on kneeling position with palms facing ground and jump forward onto your palms on the Floor and Do 4 sets and get up and Do 200 punches in 2 minutes.

(iv) Pushing the kit bag and speed punch exercise: pushing the kit bag and 2 hands punches alternatively .Do 40 sets

Saturday: Tube kicking with single leg

8th week schedule

Tube kicking with single leg 40 kicks in 45 seconds one minute or 2 minutes Rest between each single leg kicks

Do all kicks 40 times in 45 seconds each leg. Below mentioned kicks.

1. Side Kick with Left and Right Leg
2. Hook Kick with Left and Right Leg
3. Outer edge kick with Left and Right Leg
4. Round house kick with Left and Right Leg
5. *Thrust kick* with Left and Right Leg
6. Back kick with Left and Right Leg
7. Jumping Round house kick with Left and Right Leg
8. Inner edge kick with Left and Right Leg

SPEED UNDER WATER KICKS & UNDER WATER PUNCHES

Sunday 8th week schedule, water workout (water must be chest level)

I. Under water kicks Do 1 to 8 kicks each leg 15 kicks (total 30 kicks) in 1 minute
Do below mentioned kicks

1.Inner edge kick

2.Thrust kick

3.Side kick

4.Spinning kick

5.Round house kick

6. Hook kick

7. Outer edge kick

8. Hook kick and side kick with holding wall

II. a. Running in the water :
Running in the water 25 meters

b. Side Running in the water :
Running in the water right side 25 meters and left side 25 meters

c. knee raising in the water :
Knee raising in the water each leg 50 times (Total 100 times)

d. punches in the water :
(i)150 double punches in the water with alternative hands
(ii)100 single hands punches with the left hand and right hand (Total 200 punches)

e. check the speed of every individual kicks in 1 minute and make a table of improvement (minimum kicks must be 180 kicks in 1 minute in Air every week)

SQUATS KICKS

Sunday Body Weight Squats Kicks below following kicks
8th week schedule

Sit on squat and get up and kick Down heel kick with one squat 2 kicks with the Right leg and left leg and sit. Do 20 kicks each leg (i.e. Total 40 kicks)

Sit on squat and get up and kick inner edge with Right leg and left leg and sit. Do 20 kicks each leg (i.e. Total 40 kicks.

Sit on squat and get up and kick outer edge with left leg and Right leg and sit. Do 20 kicks each leg (i.e. Total 40 kicks).

Sit on squat and get up and kick front thrust kick with Right leg and with the Left leg and sit. Do 20 kicks each leg (i.e. Total 40 kicks) .

Sit on squat and get up and kick side kick with Right leg and with the Left leg and sit. Do 20 kicks each leg (i.e. Total 40 kicks).

Sit on squat and get up and kick front side kick with Right leg and with the Left leg and sit. Do 20 kicks each leg (i.e. Total 40 kicks).

Sit on squat and get up and kick Round house kick with Left leg and with the Right leg and sit. Do 20 kicks each leg (i.e. Total 40 kicks).

Sit on squat and get up and kick Back kick with Right leg and with the Left leg and sit. Do 20 kicks each leg (i.e. Total 40 kicks).

Sit on squat and get up and kick Hook kick with Left leg and with the Right leg and sit. Do 20 kicks each leg (i.e. Total 40 kicks).

SPEED TRAINING OF KICKS - BELOW 13 YEARS

Monday –I 8th week schedule

120 KICKS IN 2 MINITUES

Each kick you need to do a minimum of 60 kicks each leg in 1 minute Rest for 2 minute. Do all 1 to 10 kicks. Below mention kicks

1. down heel kick, alternative legs
2. Side Kick, alternative Legs
3. Spinning cart wheel kick, alternative legs
4. Hook Kick, alternative Legs
5. Trust Kick alternative Leg
6. Inner edge kicks alternative legs
7. Front side kicks alternative legs
8. Round House Kick Alternative Legs
9. Outer Edge Kick Alternative Legs
10. Back Kick and Do Alternative Leg

II. kick Controlling:

Do only 4 Kicks i.e., (1) Thrust Kick (2) Side Kick (3) Round House Kick (4) Back Kick

Control Each Leg at hips minimum do control for 30 to 45 seconds without any support.

III. Sitting kicks :

Do only 4 kicks (1) snap kicks (2) Side kick (3) Round house kick (4) Hook kick.
Do each kick 100 times alternative legs Lie down on back and kick continuously snap kicks start from 50 kicks to 100 kicks

Kneel Led down and sit and hands support on the ground and raise your Right leg Right side and kick side kick continuously 50 to 100 and change the leg and do with other leg same.

Kneel down and sit and hands support on the ground and kick round house kick sideways 50 to 100 times each leg.

Kneel down and sit and hands support on the ground and kick Hook kick sideways 50 to 100 times each leg.

Variation: kicks on x-ray film. You can do all kicks and all punches on x-ray film each kick 20 times and 100 punches with 2 hands.

SPEED TRAINING OF PUNCHES - BELOW 13 YEARS

Monday –I 8th week schedule

180 punches in 1 minute (Alternative Hands)

(a) Horse stand and Do 180 punches with alternative hands in 1 minute Do 2 sets.

(b) Stand in front forward stance and punch with single Right hand over the left open hand (Bend at elbow in the front) 100 punches with Single hand with in 1 minute Do 2 sets And change the hand i.e. change to left hand and punch with the same as Right hand punch.

(c) Speed sitting hand punches Sit on chair or stool and punch at least 150 times with alternative hand (with left hand and right hand) Do 2 sets.
Variation: your can do this sitting punches by blind folded i.e. with closing eyes, by imagining you are smashing with punch.

(d) Punches on x-ray film: you can practices 100 with each hand (total 200 punches)

(e) Triceps Strengthening Exercise
Keep index and thumb of each hand join together and go for pushups with leg stretch out without bending knees. Do this exercise for 10 to 20 times daily.

Friday: Same as on Monday Schedule

SPEED PEDDLE KICKS(kicking on pad)

Tuesday 8th week schedule

I. PAD KICKING EACH LEG 40 KICKS 1 TO 15 KICKS

(1) Push kick - 40 kicks each leg
(2) Front thrust kick " "
(3) Side kick " "
(4) Round house kick " "
(5) Back kick " "
(6) Outer edge kick " "
(7) Inner edge kick " "
(8) Down heel kick " "
(9) Hook kick " "
(10) Jumping side kick " "
(11) Jumping Round house kick " "

(12) Jumping Back kick - 30 kicks each leg

(13) Spin kick -40 kicks each leg

(14) Jumping spin kick -30 kicks each leg

(15) Scissor kick --40 kicks each leg

II. PAD KICKING LEFT LEG 40 KICKS IN 1MINITE SINGLE LEG

III. PAD KICKING RIGHT LEG 40 KICKS IN 1MINITE SINGLE LEG

Note: I,II and III Rest for 1 ½ minutes of each kick, Do all kicks accordingly

Thursday: Same as on Tuesday Schedule

WEDNESDAY: SPEED TRAINING OF PUNCHES

8th week schedule

(i) Knuckle pushups, Close fist and keep knuckle on ground with shoulder width distance and go down and come up or palms pushups Do 20 pushups and 100 punches in 1 minute.

(ii) Single hand knuckle or palms pushups: Do one hand knuckle pushups 15 times one hand 50 punches in 1 minute and Change knuckles. Do alternate hands Do 2 sets

(iii) Power pushups for speed & power punches
Sit on kneeling position with palms facing ground and jump forward onto your palms on the Floor and Do 3 sets and get up and Do 200 punches in 3 minutes.

(iv) Pushing the kit bag and speed punch exercise: pushing the kit bag and 2 hands punches alternatively .Do 30 sets

SPEED UNDER WATER KICKS & UNDER WATER PUNCHES

Sunday 8th week schedule, water workout (water must be chest level)

I. Under water kicks Do 1 to 8 kicks each leg 15 kicks (total 30 kicks) in 1 minute
Do below mentioned kicks

1.Inner edge kick

2.Thrust kick

3.Side kick

4.Spinning kick

5.Round house kick

6. Hook kick

7. Outer edge kick

8. Hook kick and side kick with holding wall

II. a. Running in the water :
Running in the water 20 meters

b. Side Running in the water :
Running in the water right side 20 meters and left side 20 meters

c. knee raising in the water :
Knee raising in the water each leg 40 times (Total 80 times)

d. punches in the water :
(i)100 double punches in the water with alternative hands
(ii)75 single hands punches with the left hand and right hand (Total 150 punches)

e. check every week the speed of every individual kicks in 1 minute and make a table of improvement (minimum kicks must be 180 kicks in 1 minute in Air every week)

SQUATS KICKS

Sunday Body Weight Squats Kicks below following kicks

8th week schedule

Sit on squat and get up and kick Down heel kick with one squat 2 kicks with the Right leg and left leg and sit. Do 15kicks each leg (i.e. Total 30 kicks) in 1 minute.

Sit on squat and get up and kick inner edge with Right leg and left leg and sit. Do 15 kicks each leg (i.e. Total 30 kicks) in 1 minute.

Sit on squat and get up and kick outer edge with left leg and Right leg and sit. Do 15 kicks each leg (i.e. Total 30 kicks) in 1 minute.

Sit on squat and get up and kick front thrust kick with Right leg and with the Left leg and sit. Do 15 kicks each leg (i.e. Total 30 kicks) in 1 minute.

Sit on squat and get up and kick side kick with Right leg and with the Left leg and sit. Do 15 kicks each leg (i.e. Total 30 kicks) in 1 minute.

Sit on squat and get up and kick front side kick with Right leg and with the Left leg and sit. Do 15 kicks each leg (i.e. Total 30 kicks) in 1 minute.

Sit on squat and get up and kick Round house kick with Left leg and with the Right leg and sit. Do 15 kicks each leg (i.e. Total 30 kicks) in 1 minute.

Sit on squat and get up and kick Back kick with Right leg and with the Left leg and sit. Do 15 kicks each leg (i.e. Total 30 kicks) in 1 minute.

Sit on squat and get up and kick Hook kick with Left leg and with the Right leg and sit. Do 15 kicks each leg (i.e. Total 30 kicks) in 1 minute.

QUESTION ANSWER

Advance Explosive Speed Training

1Q. Can white belt learn speed training or any specific belt?

Ans: any one can learn speed training provided he/she must know basic kicks and punch and Body conditioned so that he can avoid wear and tear.

2Q. Which style of martial arts required speed training?

Ans: any styles of martial arts including boxing, mouy thai can learn speed training.

3Q. What in the benefits of speed training?

Ans: there are several benefits, first the kicks and punches become super fast as required for Every martial arts, secondly Guinness world records you can attempts in speed kicking and speed punch thirdly your body and mind becomes so fast as you know heuro muscular exercises is very beneficial for any sport or general life.

4Q. What age do you recommended for speed training?

Ans: I recommend minimum of 10 years of age to practice speed training.

5Q can I split 7 days of speed training into 2 schedules morning and evening?

Ans: you split into 2 or 3 times in a day schedule no problem provided you must follow the Weekly schedule regularly

6Q. Do you recommend during regular martial arts class or any specific timings for speed Training.

Ans: If possible you Add in your martial arts clam schedule or else you can shift into 2 times Of schedule in the same day.

7Q. You mention 15 years above 8 weeks schedule you mean even 40 or 50 years also can Practice speed training?

Ans: yes any age he can start speed training provide he is fit enough to start with the /on week schedule.

8Q. You mentioned 1st week to 8th week schedule you mean everybody who is worth also can start from beginning or I am worth of 5th week schedule I can do easily can I start from 5th week schedule on words?

Ans: you can start at any week's schedule and check your speed at the 8th week's schedule, if not improved you can add on some more weeks of training and check the speed, you will achieve

9Q. If I am not able to reach according to the schedule the speed can be increase?

Ans: The 8th weeks Schedules are research and checked by many players if you are not able to achieve according to schedule you can add 2 more weeks to reach or achieve the required speed in kicks and punches.

10Q. If the people are overweight can it be recommend to speed training?

Ans: If you are overweight or your body has over fat or your body doesn't have flexibility or good condition then it difficult to achieve in specific time in 8 weeks. For them they must add additional training in reducing fat, achieve flexibility

11Q. How much rest I have to take after completed my weeks schedule before I jump into Other activities?

Ans: warming down or cooling down exercise are most important after you finish each schedule of the day's speed training. Further you can take massage the whole body for at least 15 to 20 minutes of every day workouts it is a serious advice for all age .

Note: warm up and warming down the body in the most important for all workouts, I caution it is dangerous if you don't follow warm up and warm down exercises for all schedules of speed training.

The World Taekwondo Federation

Citation

presented to

M. JAYANTH REDDY

in recognition of your dedicated service and outstanding contribution to the development of Taekwondo.

November 13, 2003

Un Yong Kim
President

Presidential Sports Award

Presented to

Jayanth M. Reddy

who has, through regular participation in sport,
made a commitment to the active life. My congratulations to
you on your dedication and determination.

Taekwondo
October 1998

PRESIDENT'S COUNCIL ON PHYSICAL FITNESS & SPORTS

Bill Clinton
President of the United States

Premier
KMS
KUKKIWON MEMBERSHIP SYSTEM
2019 TOP RANKED KMS DO-JANG
M. JAYANTH REDDY
Jayanth Ready International TKD Academy
The KUKKIWON certify this Taekwondo Do-jang as
2019 Top Ranked KMS Do-jang
President of the KUKKIWON
KUKKIWON

CERTIFICATE

The most roundhouse kicks executed in one minute is 171 by M. Jayanth Reddy (India) at ACN Power Gym, Hyderabad, Andhra Pradesh, India on 31 August 2010. A TaeKwonDo practitioner for more than 30 years. This confirms that you have set a new Guinness World Records achievement.

GUINNESS WORLD RECORDS LTD

CERTIFICATE

Most martial arts kicks in one hour whilst wearing 5 kg ankle weights (using alternate legs) is 2027, achieved by Jayanth Reddy (India) in Hyderabad, India, on 26 January 2018.

OFFICIALLY AMAZING™

GUINNESS WORLD RECORDS™

CERTIFICATE

The most full contact kicks in one hour by team is 106,411, and was achieved at an event organised by Jayanth Reddy (India), in Hyderabad, India, on 23 November 2018.

OFFICIALLY AMAZING™

No_ 1702001

KUKKIWON

표 창 장

LETTER OF COMMENDATION

M. JAYANTH REDDY
INDIA

위 사람은 태권도 보급 및 발전에 이바지한 공이 크므로 이 표창장을 수여합니다.

In recognition of your outstanding contribution to the development and dissemination of Taekwondo.

September 11,2017

WORLD TAEKWONDO HEADQUARTERS 국기원 KUKKIWON

국기원장 오현득

Dr. Hyun Deuk. Oh

Oh Hyun-Deuk
President of the Kukkiwon

KUKKIWON
WORLD TAEKWONDO HEADQUARTERS

32, Teheran7gil, Gangnam-gu,
Seoul, Korea (06130)

TEL +82-2-3469-0152
FAX +82-2-3469-0159

September 12, 2017

Subject: To express our heartfelt appreciation

Dear distinguished master

We would like to express our heartfelt appreciation to you for your devotion and effort to develop Taekwondo in your country.

To improve the benefit and services for our individual masters abroad, we have selected the masters who made the great achievements in Taekwondo field.

As a token of our appreciation for your efforts, we are attaching 'the Letter of Commendation'.

And there will be more souvenirs and better benefits in the coming years, so please make every endeavor to spread Taekwondo worldwide like always.

Sincerely yours,

Kukkiwon

SANGROK WORLD TAEKWONDO ACADEMY
•태권도•

표 창 장

Letter of Commendation

Name: JAYANTH REDDY MORRAMGANTI
Date of birth: 14/12/62
Country: INDIA

위 사람은 태권도 보급 및 발전에
이바지한 공이 크므로 이 증서를 수여 합니다.

In recognition of your outstanding contribution to
the development & dissemination of Sangrok Taekwondo.

30th November 2018

상록 태권도 관장 장 성 동 인

GM Chang Seong Dong
Sangrok World Taekwondo Academy

주하이데라바드명예영사관
Honorary Consulate General of the Republic of Korea in Hyderabad

Certificate Of Appreciation

Presented to

Mr. M. Jayanth Reddy, Grand Master

8th Dan for his outstanding contribution and dedicated service to the development of Taekwondo and it's culture.

Date: 09.01.2019

Suresh Chukkapalli
Honorary Consul General

KUKKIWON
WORLD TAEKWONDO HEADQUARTERS

29th October, 2018

Letter of Invitation

Dear : M. JAYANTH REDDY Kukkiwon Advisory Committee Member

Date of Birth: 14 – Dec – 1962
Passport No.: H7483302

It is an honor for KUKKIWON, World Taekwondo Headquarters to invite respectful masters to the "8th Seoul Global Taekwondo Leader's Forum".
We would like to have an opportunity to ruminate on humanism in the perspective of Taekwondo.
The Forum will be held from 25th to 26th November, 2018 in Le Meridien Hotel Seoul.

We are planning to appoint Kukkiwon Advisory Committee for the duration of the event.
We will re-appoint the existing members and appoint new members among the participants.

* Accommodation is provided in Novotel Ambassador Seoul Gangnam.

Sincerely Yours,

Dr. Hyun Deuk Oh

Ph.D. Oh Hyun Deuk

President of Kukkiwon
World Taekwondo Headquarter

KUKKIWON
635 Yuksam-dong Gangnam-gu, Seoul, 135-908 Korea www.kukkiwon.or.kr
Tel: +82-2-3469-0153 E-mail: 2017tkdforum@gmail.com